# Primary Partners®

# Teaching Tools

## For Sharing Time and Family Home Evenings

THEME: I Belong to The Church of Jesus Christ
of Latter-day Saints

WRITTEN BY MARY H. ROSS - ILLUSTRATED BY JENNETTE GUYMON-KING

## Introducing the Author and Illustrator, Creators of the Following Series of Books and CD-ROMS:

*Primary Partners®* manual match activities, sharing time, singing fun, and Achievement Days, *Young Women Fun-tastic! Activities for Manuals 1-3 and Personal Progress Motivators, Gospel Fun Activities, Super Singing Activities, Super Little Singers, File Folder Family Home Evenings*, and *Home-spun Fun Family Home Evenings*

Mary Ross, Author

Mary Ross is an energetic mother, and has been a Primary teacher, and Achievement Days leader. She loves to help children and young women have a good time while learning. She has studied acting, modeling, and voice. Her varied interests include writing, creating activities and children's parties, and cooking. Mary and her husband, Paul, live with their daughter, Jennifer, in Sandy, Utah.

Jennette Guymon-King, Illustrator

Jennette Guymon-King has studied graphic arts and illustration at Utah Valley College and the University of Utah. She served a mission to Japan. Jennette enjoys sports, reading, cooking, art, gardening, and freelance illustrating. Jennette and her husband Clayton, live in Riverton, Utah. They are the proud parents of their daughter Kayla Mae, and sons Levi and Carson.

Copyright © 2002 by Mary H. Ross and Jennette Guymon-King
All Rights Reserved

Covenant Communications, Inc.
American Fork, Utah

Printed in Canada
First Printing: November 2002

**COPYRIGHT NOTICE:** Patterns in this book are for use by individual Primaries and individual families only. Copying patterns for another use is prohibited.

*Primary Partners®* Teaching Tools: I Belong to The Church of Jesus Christ of Latter-day Saints
ISBN 1-59156-143-4

ACKNOWLEDGEMENTS: Thanks to Inspire Graphics (www.inspiregraphics.com) for the use of Lettering Delights computer fonts. —This product is neither sponsored nor endorsed by The Church of Jesus Christ of Latter-day Saints.

# INTRODUCTION

## Primary Partners
# TEACHING TOOLS
### for Sharing Time and Family Home Evenings
### Theme: I Belong to The Church of Jesus Christ of Latter-day Saints

*I Belong to The Church of Jesus Christ of Latter-day Saints* can be a fun and exciting theme to teach with the right *teaching tools*. This book contains 66 activities to help make learning fun. You can suggest them to your Primary teachers for class presentations or use them to add to and enhance your own sharing time or family home evening presentations. Plus, using them for family home evening will help reinforce what children are learning in Primary.

With each sharing time theme, the Church recommends certain Primary lessons that will add to your sharing time presentations. This book provides learning activities that match each of these Primary lessons and more. These activities can also be found in the eight volumes of *Primary Partners* lesson-match activity books.

Here you will find activities that coordinate with each of the twelve sharing time themes for the year 2003: I Belong to The Church of Jesus Christ of Latter-day Saints. The illustrations for the activities can be enlarged to present in large groups, such as sharing time, or can be copied as they are to present in classrooms, family home evening, or as handouts.

The activities in this book are also available on CD-ROM to print images in color and black and white (shown right).

The *Teaching Tools* activities coordinate with the Primary lessons which give you ideas for lesson presentations. Example: the *Premortal Life Puppet Show* on page 1 (shown left) refers to scripture story and discussions on pages 17-18 in the *Primary 2-CTR A Manual*.

You will find more learning activities for the "I Belong to The Church of Jesus Christ of Latter-day Saints" 2003 themes in the back of this book. Example: The *Primary Partners Sharing Time* (12 theme activities), *Gospel Fun Activities* (12 theme activities in full-color, ready to use), and *Primary Partners Singing Fun!*, and more.

# Table of Contents

Teaching Tools — 2003 Sharing Time Theme:
I Belong to The Church of Jesus Christ of Latter-day Saints

---

### Theme 1: I Belong to The Church of Jesus Christ — 3 Nephi 26:21

1. I Chose to Follow Jesus (Premortal Life Puppet Show) .................................................. 1, 4-5
2. My Faith Grows As I Obey (Premortal Life, Earth Life Quiz) ........................................ 1, 6
3. The Mission of Jesus Christ (Review Game) ............................................................... 2, 7-8
4. Heavenly Keys (Priesthood Keys Crossword Puzzle) ................................................... 2, 9
5. The Apostles Were Special Witnesses of Jesus Christ (Apostle Match Game) .......... 3, 10
6. Jesus Christ's Church Is Restored (Apostasy Mirror Puzzle Teaching Tool) ............. 3, 11-12

---

### Theme 2: I Belong to The Church of Jesus Christ of Latter-day Saints — D&C 115:4

1. Joseph Smith Saw Heavenly Father and Jesus (Sacred Grove Movable Scene) ......... 13, 18
2. Fulness of the Gospel—Angel Moroni's Good News Message (Moroni's Match Game) ... 14, 19-20
3. The Priesthood Blesses My Life (Priesthood Pockets Puzzle) ..................................... 14, 21
4. Priesthood Ordinances Restored (Ordinance Opportunity Game) .............................. 15, 22-23
5. The True Church Was Restored to the Earth (Then and Now Match Game) ............ 16, 24
6. Jesus Christ's Church Restored (Membership Window Wheel) .................................. 17, 25-26
7. I Promise and Heavenly Father Promises (Puzzles) ................................................... 17, 27

---

### Theme 3: I Know Who I Am — Psalm 82:6

1. I Can Recognize and Seek True Gifts (Gifts of the Spirit Cross Match) ..................... 28, 30
2. I Will Use My Talents to Serve Others (Service and Talent Show Poster) ................. 28, 31
3. I Will Show Love to Others as I Serve (My Circle of Love Spin-and-Serve Game) .... 29, 32
4. I Can Be Happy As I Serve (Service Station Sack of Reminders) ............................... 29, 33

---

### Theme 4: I Believe in the Savior, Jesus Christ — Matthew 16:16

1. Jesus Suffered for Me (Atonement Ponder Wheel) ..................................................... 34, 37-38
2. I Can Live in Heaven (Alma the Younger's Road to Repentance Maze) .................... 35, 39
3. Jesus Helped Me Overcome Sin and Death (Repentance Puzzle) ............................... 35, 40
4. The Holy Ghost Will Guide and Comfort Me (Invite the Spirit Choice Game) .......... 36, 41-42
5. Happiness Comes From Choosing the Right (CTR Happiness Wheel) ....................... 36, 43-44

## Theme 5: The Prophet Speaks for the Savior. I Can Follow the Prophet Today – D&C 1:38

1. I Know the Prophet Lives (Prophet Poster Fold-out Pictures) . . . . . . . . . . . . . . . . . . . . . . . . 45, 49
2. I Will Listen to the Prophet to Stay in the Light (Cycle of History Wheel) . . . . . . . . . . 46, 50-51
3. The Prophet Speaks and I Listen (Revelation Routes) . . . . . . . . . . . . . . . . . . . . . . . . . . . 47, 52
4. Prophets Tell Me About the Life and Mission of Jesus (Prophet Presentation) . . . . . . . 47, 53-54
5. The Prophets Give Latter-day Revelation (Standard Works Think-athon) . . . . . . . . . . . 48, 55-57

## Theme 6: I Know God's Plan – Moses 1:39

1. Jesus Gave Me Immortality and Eternal Life (Atonement Object Lesson) . . . . . . . . . . . . . 58, 63
2. Heavenly Father's Plan Is for Me (Plan of Salvation Storyboard and Quiz) . . . . . . . . . 59, 64-65
3. Heavenly Father Trusts Us to Follow (Heaven Road Map) . . . . . . . . . . . . . . . . . . . . . . . . 59, 66
4. Heavenly Father Gave Me Free Agency (Choices Slap Game) . . . . . . . . . . . . . . . . . . . 60, 67-68
5. I Will Show Heavenly Father and Jesus Respect (Respectful Choices Poster) . . . . . . . 60, 69-70
6. My Testimony of Jesus (What Would Jesus Do? Choice Situation Sack) . . . . . . . . . . . . . . 61, 71
7. I Will Live the Gospel of Jesus Christ (Faithful Footsteps Goal Flip Chart) . . . . . . . . . 61, 72-74
8. Jesus Christ Was Chosen to Be My Savior (Choices & Consequences Match Game) . . . . 62, 75-76
9. I Can Be like Jesus (Compassion Wheel) . . . . . . . . . . . . . . . . . . . . . . . . . . . . . . . . . . . . 62, 77-78

## Theme 7: I'll Follow Him in Faith – Galatians 3:26

1. Heavenly Father Helps Me as I Pray in Faith (My Personal Goliaths Prayer Journal) . . . . . 79, 81
2. I Will Seek Heavenly Father's Guidance (Puzzled About Prayer Crossword Puzzle) . . . . . . 79, 82
3. Jesus Christ Performed Miracles (Three Miracles Picture Poster) . . . . . . . . . . . . . . . . . 80, 83-84
4. I Will Read the Scriptures and Keep the Commandments (Sticker Challenge) . . . . . . . 80, 85-86

## Theme 8: I'll Honor His Name – Mosiah 5:8

1. I Will Be Valiant and Tell Others About Jesus (Choice Situation Sack) . . . . . . . . . . . . . . . 87, 71
2. I Will Think of Jesus (Testimony Building Blocks Puzzle) . . . . . . . . . . . . . . . . . . . . . . . . . 87, 90
3. I Will Remember Jesus (Sacrament Symbols Puzzles) . . . . . . . . . . . . . . . . . . . . . . . . . . . . 88, 91
4. Heavenly Father Helps Me as I Obey (Commandment Concentration) . . . . . . . . . . . . . . . 88, 92
5. I Honor Heavenly Father, Jesus Christ, and the Holy Ghost (Worship Word Find) . . . . . . 89, 93

### Theme 9   I'll Do What is Right – Deuteronomy 6:18

1. Jesus Speaks to Me Through the Holy Ghost (Spirit of Truth Cross Match) . . . . . . . . . . . . 94, 97
2. I Will Live Worthy to Receive Priesthood Blessings
   (My Gospel Standards Sentence Search) . . . . . . . . . . . . . . . . . . . . . . . . . . . . . . . . . . . . . . 94, 98
3. I Will Make and Keep Good Promises (Honesty Pays Blessings Bucks Game) . . . . . . . . 95, 99-100
4. I Can Be a True Friend to Jesus & Others (Fishing for a Friend Spin-and-Tell) . . . . . 95, 101-102
5. I Will Be a Positive Influence on My Friends (Peer Pressure Cross Match Puzzle) . . . . . . 96, 103
6. I Will Keep This Law of Health (Word of Wisdom Choices Match Puzzle) . . . . . . . . . . . . 96, 104

### Theme 10   I'll Follow His Light – John 14:6

1. I Will Follow Jesus (Footstep Flash Cards) . . . . . . . . . . . . . . . . . . . . . . . . . . . . . . 105, 108-109
2. Others Testify That Jesus Is God's Son
   (Testimonies of Jesus Scripture Picture Match Game) . . . . . . . . . . . . . . . . . . . . . 105, 110-111
3. Jesus Taught Us How to Return to Heaven ("Bee"-atitude Cross Match) . . . . . . . . . . . . 106, 112
4. The Gospel of Jesus Christ Is My Sure Foundation (Rock and Body Puzzle) . . . . . . . . . . 106, 113
5. I Can Follow Jesus and Obey (Heavenly Treasure Hunt) . . . . . . . . . . . . . . . . . . . . . . . . . 107, 114
6. The Armor of God Will Protect Me from Evil (Fight for Right! Word Choice) . . . . . . . . 107, 115

### Theme 11   Teachings of the Prophet – Amos 3:7

1. I Will Listen to the Prophet (The Prophet Guides Choices & Consequences Cross Match). . 116, 118
2. I Will Trust in the Lord and Obey (Follow Righteous Leaders Trust-and-Tell Game) . . . . . 116, 119
3. On the Right Road to Happiness (Valiantville "Convert"-able Obstacle Course) . . . . . . . . 117, 120
4. The Gospel of Jesus Christ Is True (Valiant Testimony Board Game) . . . . . . . . . . . . 117, 121-123

### Theme 12   His Truth I Will Proclaim – Mosiah 18:9

1. I Will Be Valiant and Testify of Jesus (Valiant Testimony Balloon Maze) . . . . . . . . . . . . 124, 127
2. I Will Prepare Now to Share the Gospel with Others
   (Missionary Mystery! Word Search) . . . . . . . . . . . . . . . . . . . . . . . . . . . . . . . . . . . . . . . . . 125, 128
3. I Will Prepare for My Mission (Missionary Doors Scripture Search) . . . . . . . . . . . . . . . . 125, 129
4. Heavenly Father Wants Everyone to Learn the Gospel
   (My Mission Statement Message Decoder) . . . . . . . . . . . . . . . . . . . . . . . . . . . . . . . . . . . 126, 130
5. I Can "Bear" My Testimony (Secret Message Poster) . . . . . . . . . . . . . . . . . . . . . . . . . . . 126, 131

### More Learning Activities for the "I Belong to The Church of Jesus Christ of Latter-day Saints" 2003 Themes and More

. . . . . . . . . . . . . . . . . . . . . . . . . . . . . . . . . . . . . . . . . . . . . . . . . . . . . . . . . . . . . . . . . . . . . . . . . . 132-138

# Theme 1: I Belong to The Church of Jesus Christ—3 Nephi 26:21

**SONG:** Sing "The Church of Jesus Christ," *Children's Songbook*, page 77. This song is illustrated in *Primary Partners Singing Fun! I Belong to The Church of Latter-day Saints* book and CD-ROM.

Ask: "Why are we baptized in the name of Jesus Christ? Why do we belong to His Church?" Answer the questions, using the scriptures, Primary lessons, and sources below to teach.

> **Heavenly Father Loves and Blesses Us. He Sent His Son, Jesus Christ to Earth to Be Our Savior** (John 3:16; *Primary 1*, lesson 6; *Primary 6*, lesson 2).

## Sharing Time Activity 1:
### I Chose to Follow Jesus (Premortal Life Puppet Show)

**TO MAKE:** *Copy/enlarge, color, and cut out the *Premortal Life Puppet Show* (pages 4-5). Tape puppets on wooden craft sticks to show.

**PREPARATION:** Review lesson 4 and the scripture story and discussions (pages 17-18) in the *Primary 2—CTR A Manual*.

**ACTIVITY:** Create a premortal life puppet show. Then role-play our premortal life where we lived with Heavenly Father and Jesus. Role-play, moving puppets across the premortal life scene to show that we chose to follow Jesus.
*Ideas:* Job 38:7—we shouted for joy when Heavenly Father told us He was going to send someone (Jesus Christ) to help us; Moses 4:1-4—Satan became the devil, tempting Adam and Eve, and death entered the world; Abraham 3:24-28—Heavenly Father sent Jesus to help us; we are on earth today, which means we chose to follow Jesus; see Article of Faith 1, *Gospel Principles*, chapter 3, and song, "He Sent His Son," *Children's Songbook*, 34.

## Sharing Time Activity 2:
### My Faith Grows as I Obey (Premortal Life, Earth Life Quiz)

**TO MAKE:** *Copy/enlarge, color, and cut out the *Premortal Life, Earth Life Quiz* (page 6). *Fun Idea:* Cut out a plastic doll using plastic sheet protectors and paper doll pattern (cut head on fold line). Plastic spirit should have two sides to slip over paper doll when showing how spirit enters and leaves the body.

**PREPARATION:** Review lesson 28 and enrichment activity 2 (page 157) in the *Primary 5 Doctrine and Covenants/Church History Manual*.

**ACTIVITY:** Tell children that their faith grows as they make right choices. Have them think about the choice we made to come to earth and write it in the premortal circle. Then think about the choices we make on earth to pass the test and return to our heavenly home. *Option:* Use as a teaching tool. Cut out the arrow, circles, and children to show the bodies moving from premortal life to earth life. If using plastic spirit (see above), slide the plastic over a body to demonstrate how the spirit is in premortal life and then comes to earth to gain a body (sliding the plastic over the body).

*All images can be printed in full color or black and white using the CD-ROM:
Primary Partners Teaching Tools—I Belong to The Church of Jesus Christ of Latter-day Saints.

## Sharing Time Activity 3:
### The Mission of Jesus Christ (Review Game)

**TO MAKE:** *Copy/enlarge, color, and cut out the *Mission of Jesus Christ Review Game* (pages 7-8). Place wordstrips on the board lengthwise so cards can be placed below wordstrips.

**PREPARATION:** Review lesson 35 and enrichment activity 3 (page 122) in the *Primary 7 New Testament Manual*.

**ACTIVITY:** Read to children the mission statement Jesus Christ gave to Moses (Moses 1:39 on poster, page 74): "Behold, this is my work and my glory—to bring to pass the immortality and eternal life of man." Then play these review games to learn how Jesus fulfilled His mission before, during, and after His life on this Earth.

***To Play Review Game:*** (1) Divide group into two teams. Give each team eight cards with tape on the back (to mount on the wall). (2) Take turns placing the card under the matching wordstrip. If the match is correct, the team receives 10 points. The first team to win 100 points wins first game.

***Answers:*** Place the following numbered cards under the wordstrips: "Christ's Premortal Life" (3, 11, 14, 16) "Christ's Mortal Life" (1, 6, 7, 12, 2) "Christ's Life After Death" (5, 15, 9, 13, 4, 10, 8)

---

**Jesus Organized His Church. He Ordained Others to the Priesthood to Act in His Name**
(Matthew 16:19; *Primary 7*, lesson 15).

---

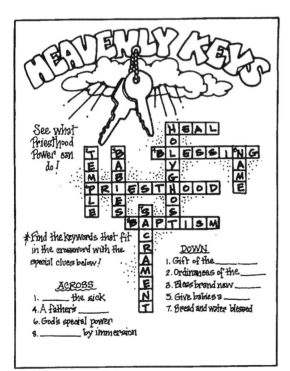

## Sharing Time Activity 4: Heavenly Keys
### (Priesthood Keys Crossword Puzzle)

**TO MAKE:** *Copy/enlarge and color the *Priesthood Keys Crossword Puzzle* (page 9).

**PREPARATION:** Review lesson 15 and enrichment activity 1 (page 52) in the *Primary 7 New Testament Manual*.

**ACTIVITY:** Help children learn about the power of the priesthood by completing this puzzle. The word "PRIESTHOOD" is found in the center and all the other words describe the special powers and blessings that come from the priesthood.

***Answers:*** Across: 1. heal, 4. blessing, 6. priesthood, 8. baptism. Down: 1. Holy Ghost, 2. temple, 3. babies, 5. name, 7. sacrament.

**The New Testament Teaches Us about Christ's Church**
(Article of Faith 6; *Primary 7*, lesson 9; *Gospel Principles*, chapter 16).

## Sharing Time Activity 5:
### The Apostles Were Special Witnesses of Jesus Christ (Apostle Match Game)

**TO MAKE:** *Copy/enlarge, color, and cut out two sets of *Apostle Match Game* cards (page 10).

**PREPARATION:** Review lesson 9 and enrichment activity 2 (page 31) in the *Primary 7 New Testament Manual*.

**ACTIVITY:** Play the *Apostles Match Game* to learn about the 12 Apostles that Jesus chose to lead His church. Talk about the Apostles chosen. Explain that the Apostles were teachers, examples, and special witnesses of Jesus Christ. They followed Jesus and taught others about the plan of salvation. They taught what He taught, they wrote about Him in the scriptures. They tried to live as He did.

**To Play:** (1) Divide group into two teams. (2) Lay cards facedown. (3) Teams take turns drawing two cards to make a match. When a match is made, say the two Apostles' names aloud. (4) When all cards are matched, the team with the most matches wins. (5) If the cards "Special Witness of Jesus" or "Teacher/Example" are matched, take another turn.

---

**When People Began to Change Jesus' Teachings, Many Fell Away from His Church (Apostasy). The Apostles Were Killed, and the Lord Withdrew His Priesthood Authority**
(Joseph Smith—History 1:19; D&C 1:15; *Primary 5*, lesson 2).

## Sharing Time Activity 6: Jesus Christ's Church Is Restored (Apostasy Mirror Puzzle Teaching Tool)

**TO MAKE:** *Copy/enlarge, color, and cut out the *Apostasy Mirror Puzzle Teaching Tool* (page 11) on colored cardstock paper. *Option:* *Copy/enlarge and cut out the two-sided card (page 12) showing the *Apostasy Mirror* verse and mirror for each child to take home.

**PREPARATION:** Review lesson 2 and the scriptural and historical accounts (pages 8-9) and suggested family sharing (page 11) in the *Primary 5 Doctrine and Covenants/Church History Manual*.

**ACTIVITY:** Talk about the Apostasy and Restoration of the Church of Jesus Christ as you put up and take down this puzzle. Read the *Apostasy Mirror* (page 12) to children and show puzzle.

---

*All images can be printed in full color or black and white using the CD-ROM:
Primary Partners Teaching Tools—I Belong to The Church of Jesus Christ of Latter-day Saints.*

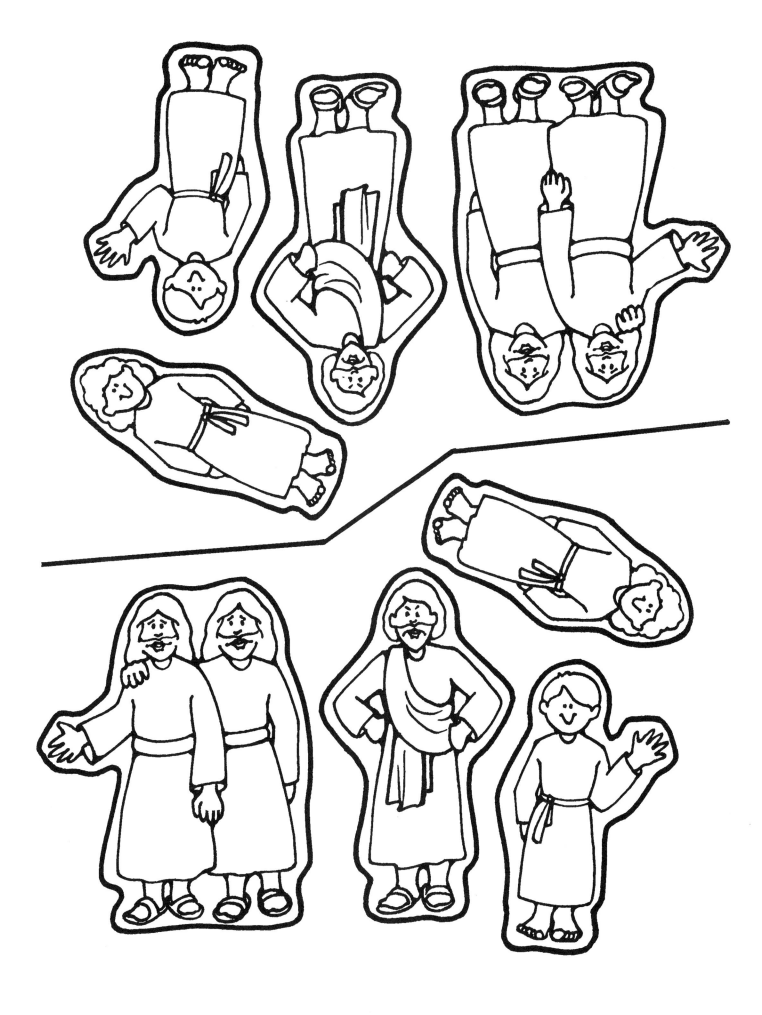

Christ's Premortal Life

Christ's Mortal Life

Christ's Life After Death

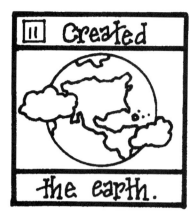

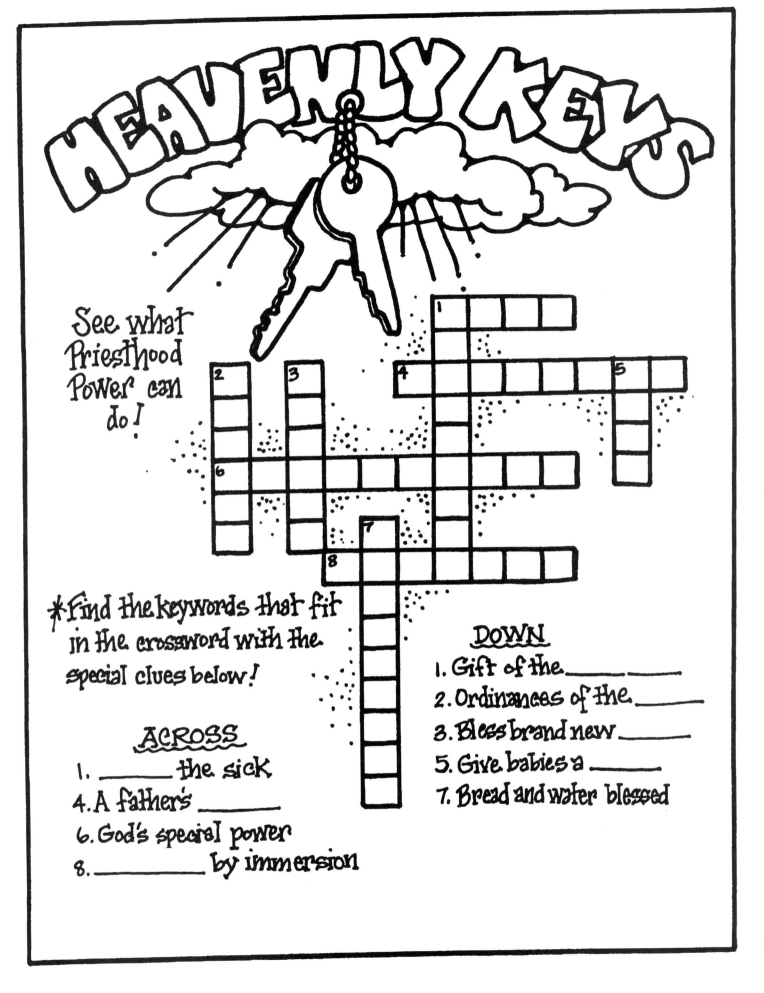

# Apostasy Mirror

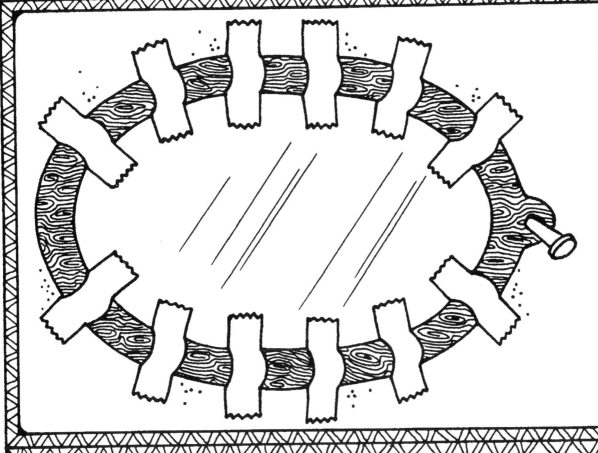

## The Apostasy Mirror

This mirror represents the Church of Jesus Christ. The mirror represents the Church itself, with Christ at the top as the nail, and each of the Apostles as a piece of tape. When Christ died, the Apostles held up the mirror and took care of the affairs of the Church. When the Apostles were killed, the mirror fell and broke, thus resulting in the Apostasy. But people still saw good in the mirror and took pieces and built around them, resulting in the many churches of today. This exemplifies the reason we needed a Restoration and not just a reformation... because a mirror that has been broken cannot be repaired — it must be replaced.

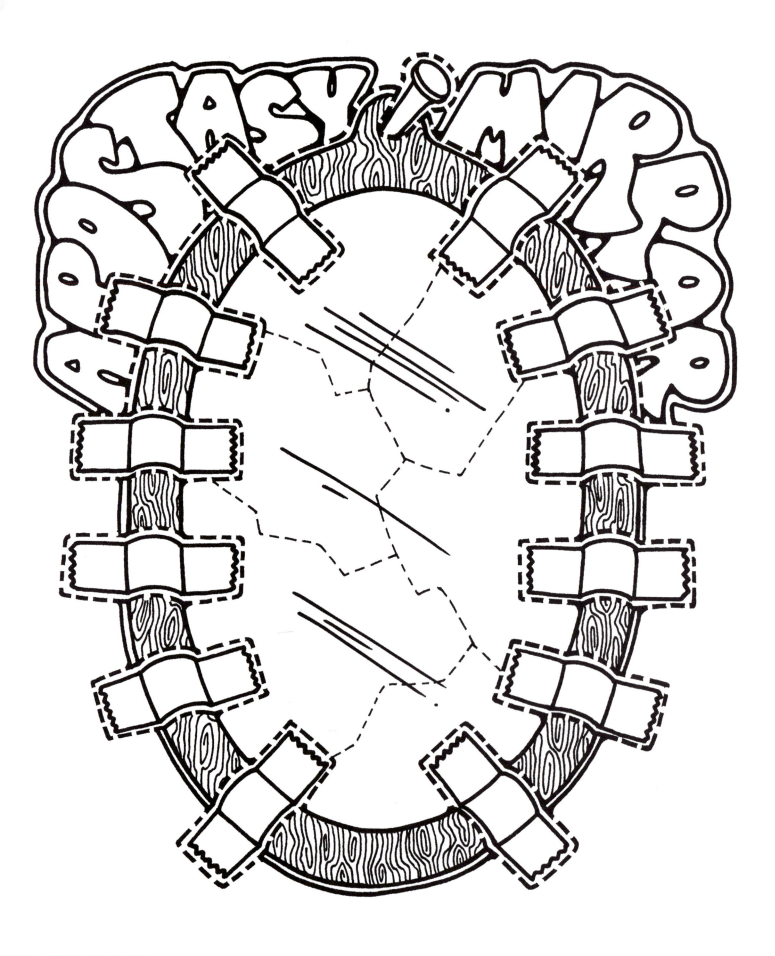

# Theme 2: I Belong to The Church of Jesus Christ of Latter-day Saints—D&C 115:4

**SONG:** Sing "On a Golden Springtime," *Children's Songbook*, page 88. This song is illustrated in *Primary Partners Singing Fun! I Belong to The Church of Latter-day Saints* book and CD-ROM.

Ask: "What do we mean when we say we belong to The Church of Jesus Christ of Latter-day Saints?" Answer the question, using the scriptures, Primary lessons, and sources below to teach.

> **In the First Vision, Joseph Smith Saw God the Father and His Son, Jesus Christ. He Learned That Christ's True Church Would Be Restored in These Latter-days**
> (Articles of Faith 1, 6; Joseph Smith—History 1:7-20; *Primary 5*, lesson 1).

## Sharing Time Activity 1: Joseph Smith Saw Heavenly Father and Jesus (Sacred Grove Movable Scene)

**TO MAKE:** *Copy, color, and cut out the *Sacred Grove Movable Scene* with Heavenly Father and Jesus, and Joseph Smith (page 18). Glue Joseph Smith sticker in place. Poke two holes with a pencil. Place page reinforcements over holes on back. Thread string through holes and tie a knot in front. Tape the knot on the back of Heavenly Father and Jesus images.

**PREPARATION:** Review lesson 5 and the picture and discussion (pages 21-22) in the *Primary 3-CTR B Manual*.

**ACTIVITY:** Tell about Joseph Smith praying in the grove of trees, and seeing Heavenly Father and Jesus. As you tell the story, have a child place Joseph Smith in the grove when it comes to that part in the story. Have another child move the Heavenly Father and Jesus images up and down as They speak to him. Children can visualize this scene if they have a chance to participate by using this movable Sacred Grove scene. Talk to children about how Joseph Smith, at such an early age, saw the Savior Jesus Christ and Heavenly Father. Because of his great faith and desire to know the truth, he had this experience.

*All images can be printed in full color or black and white using the CD-ROM: Primary Partners Teaching Tools—I Belong to The Church of Jesus Christ of Latter-day Saints.*

Primary Partners Teaching Tools — I Belong to The Church — Theme 2

**Joseph Smith Was Called to Be a Prophet. He Translated the Book of Mormon, Which Contains the Fulness of the Gospel** (Article of Faith 8; D&C 124:125; *Primary 3*, lesson 15).

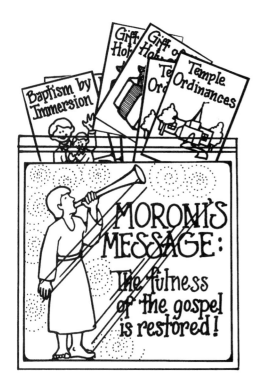

**Sharing Time Activity 2:** *Fulness of the Gospel—Angel Moroni's Good News Message (Moroni's Match Game)*

**TO MAKE:** *Copy, color, and cut out the *Moroni's Match Game* (pages 19-20), making two sets of the cards.

**PREPARATION:** Review lesson 3 and enrichment activity 3 (page 14) in the *Primary 5 Doctrine and Covenants Manual*.

**ACTIVITY:** Tell children about the Prophet Joseph Smith, who restored the fulness of the gospel. The Angel Moroni brought the good news of the gospel to Joseph Smith. When children play this game they will learn the basic elements of the gospel restored to the Prophet Joseph Smith. Talk about each card as you show it.

*To Play:* Tape the "Moroni's Message" sign on the board and the cards facedown on the board, placed randomly. Divide children into two teams. Have the teams take turns turning two cards over for all to see and name the gospel basics. When a match is made, set aside matching cards. The team with the most matches wins.

**The Priesthood, Ordinances, and Doctrines Were Restored by Heavenly Messengers and Revelation** (Articles of Faith 5, 9; D&C 13:1; *Primary 5*, lessons 8, 12).

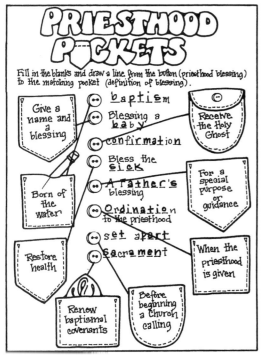

**Sharing Time Activity 3:** *The Priesthood Blesses My Life (Priesthood Pockets Puzzle)*

**TO MAKE:** *Copy, color, and cut out the *Priesthood Pockets Puzzle* (page 21). If doing two sharing times, make an additional copy, as children will mark on this one.

**PREPARATION:** Review lesson 33 and enrichment activity 1 (page 146) in the *Primary 6 Old Testament Manual*.

**ACTIVITY:** Help children learn how the priesthood power can bless their lives by matching the blessing with the definition. Fill in the blanks and draw a line from the button to the matching pocket.

*All images can be printed in full color or black and white using the CD-ROM: Primary Partners Teaching Tools—I Belong to The Church of Jesus Christ of Latter-day Saints.

### Sharing Time Activity 4: Priesthood Ordinances Restored (Ordinance Opportunity Game)

**TO MAKE:** *Copy, color, and cut out the *Ordinance Opportunity Game* board, "MOVE" numbers, and team markers (pages 22-23).

**PREPARATION:** Review lesson 12, attention activity (page 57), and enrichment activity 2 (page 61) in the *Primary 5 Doctrine and Covenants Manual.*

**ACTIVITY:**
1. Review the *Ordinance Opportunity Game* board, telling children there are certain ordinances that help us return to our heavenly home to live with Heavenly Father again someday.
2. Point to the START position and say, "We are heaven sent." Talk about Heavenly Father and Jesus' plan to send us here to the earth to be tried and tested.
3. Explain that as we learn to make right choices, we can participate in the ordinance of baptism and be confirmed a member of The Church of Jesus Christ of Latter-day Saints and receive the Holy Ghost to guide us. As we continue to

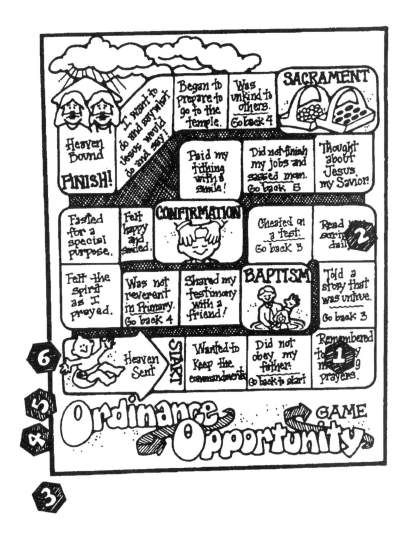

keep the commandments, we can be worthy to partake of the ordinance of the sacrament. As we keep the commandments, we can prepare to go to the temple to partake of the ordinances of endowments and sealing so we can be with our families forever. Then as we finish our life here on earth, we can be part of Heavenly Father's kingdom.

**To Play:** Help children find their way back to their heavenly home by moving forward on the game board, trying to land on the right choices instead of the wrong.
1. Divide children into two teams using the #1 and 2 markers, or have up to 12 players play using the #1-12 markers. Place double-stick tape or fun tack of the back of each marker to move across the game board.
2. Take turns drawing "MOVE" numbers from a bowl or hat and moving the spaces designated from the START position.
3. Move along the game board, placing markers on board. If children make a wrong choice move, their team moves back instead of forward (or player moves back, if playing individually).
4. The first team or individual to reach heaven wins!

*All images can be printed in full color or black and white using the CD-ROM:
*Primary Partners Teaching Tools—I Belong to The Church of Jesus Christ of Latter-day Saints.*

Primary Partners Teaching Tools — I Belong to The Church — Theme 2

### Sharing Time Activity 5: The True Church Was Restored to the Earth (Then and Now Match Game)

**TO MAKE:** *Copy, color, and cut out two sets of *Then and Now Match Game* cards (page 24).

**PREPARATION:** Review lesson 11 and enrichment activities 3, 5, and 6 (pages 54-55) in the *Primary 5 Doctrine and Covenants Manual*.

**ACTIVITY:** Help children compare the gospel of Jesus Christ *then* (when Jesus came to earth), and *now* (when Joseph Smith restored the gospel in these latter days). (1) Read the scriptures and show Then and Now cards to learn about then and now detailed below. (2) Play the game detailed below.

*Then*—Sermon on the Mount — Matthew 5:6
    (Christ begins his ministry)
*Now*—First Vision — D&C 115:4, D&C 21:1, 3-4
    (Christ restores His Church to the earth)

*Then*—Jesus was baptized — Matthew 3:13, 16
*Now*—We are baptized — D&C 20:72-74

*Then*—Jesus ordained Apostles — Ephesians 2:19-20
    (so Apostles could administer the priesthood),
*Now*—Melchizedek Priesthood restored — D&C 21:1
    (so priesthood power can again be on the
    earth) D&C 27:12 (128:20)

*Then*—Sacrament: Jesus blesses — Luke 22:19-20
*Now*—Sacrament: Members partake — D&C 20:75

*Then*—Jesus Christ is head of the Church — Amos 3:7
*Now*—Jesus Christ is head of the Church — D&C 21:5

**To Play the Match Game:**
Divide children into two teams. Mix cards and lay each card facedown on the floor or table. Children sit in a circle to play. Take turns turning two cards over for all to see, saying "then" and/or "now" as they read: Baptism by Immersion ("then/now"), the Last Supper ("then"), Sacrament ("now"), etc. When a match is made, the child collects matching cards. The team with the most matches wins.

*All images can be printed in full color or black and white using the CD-ROM: *Primary Partners Teaching Tools—I Belong to The Church of Jesus Christ of Latter-day Saints.*

## Sharing Time Activity 6:
### Jesus Christ's Church Restored (Membership Window Wheel)

**TO MAKE:** *Copy, color, and cut out the *Membership Window Wheel* (pages 25-26). Attach part A on top of part B with a paper fastener or a metal or button brad. *To make button brad:* Sew two buttons together on opposite sides (threading thread through the same hole in the paper) to attach window wheels.

**PREPARATION:** Review lesson 6 and the review the chalkboard discussion (page 27) in the *Primary 3—CTR B Manual.*

**ACTIVITY:** Turn the wheel to show and talk about reasons we want to be a member of The Church of Jesus Christ of Latter-day Saints.

## Sharing Time Activity 7:
### I Promise and Heavenly Father Promises (Puzzle)

**TO MAKE:** *Copy, color, and cut out the *I Promise* two-sided puzzle (page 27).

**PREPARATION:** Review lesson 13 and the wordstrips and discussion (page 63) in the *Primary 3—CTR B Manual.*

**ACTIVITY:** Help children remember the promises they make to Heavenly Father at baptism and the promises Heavenly Father makes to them when they are baptized. To show children, make a puzzle cutting the puzzle in half on the fold line. Tape the "I Promise" sign on the left of a poster or board and the "Heavenly Father Promises" sign on the right. Tape wordstrips randomly on the board. Have children take turns coming up, finding a wordstrip and placing it under the matching promise sign.

*All images can be printed in full color or black and white using the CD-ROM: Primary Partners Teaching Tools—I Belong to The Church of Jesus Christ of Latter-day Saints.

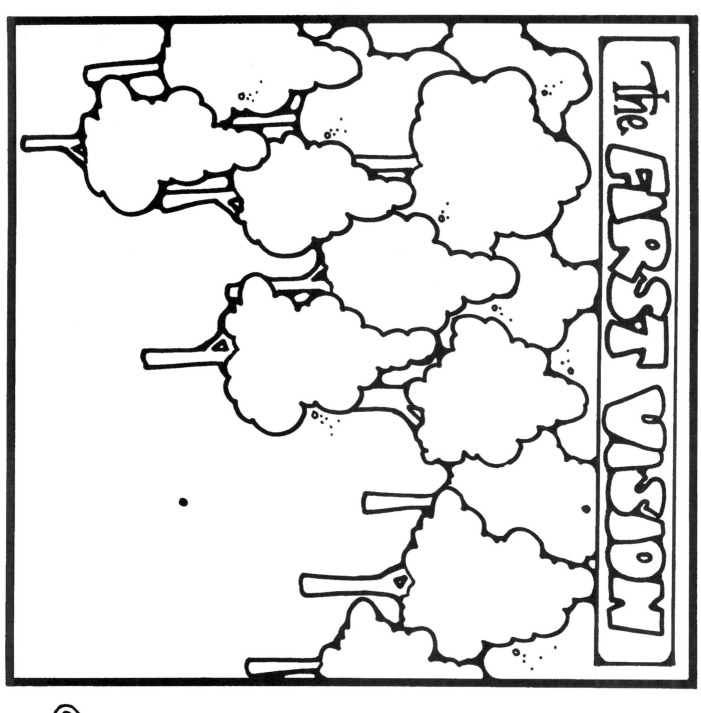
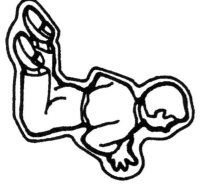

# PRIESTHOOD POCKETS

Fill in the blanks and draw a line from the button (priesthood blessing) to the matching pocket (definition of blessing).

**Give a name and a blessing**

**Receive the Holy Ghost**

- ⊙ _ a _ _ _ _ _ m
- ⊙ Blessing a _ _ b _
- ⊙ c _ _ f _ _ _ _ _ _ io _
- ⊙ Bless the _ _ _ _
- ⊙ A F _ _ _ _ _ _ ' _ blessing
- ⊙ _ r _ _ _ _ _ _ _ _ n to the priesthood
- ⊙ s _ _ a _ _ _ _ _
- ⊙ _ _ cr _ _ _ _ _ t

**Born of the water**

**For a special purpose or guidance**

**Restore health**

**When the priesthood is given**

**Renew baptismal covenants**

**Before beginning a Church calling**

| MOVE ① | MOVE ② | MOVE ③ | MOVE ④ | MOVE ⑤ |
|---|---|---|---|---|
| MOVE ① | MOVE ② | MOVE ③ | MOVE ④ | MOVE ⑤ |
| MOVE ① | MOVE ② | MOVE ③ | MOVE ④ | MOVE ⑤ |
| MOVE ① | MOVE ② | MOVE ③ | MOVE ④ | MOVE ⑤ |
| MOVE ① | MOVE ② | MOVE ③ | MOVE ④ | MOVE ⑤ |
| MOVE ① | MOVE ② | MOVE ③ | MOVE ④ | MOVE ⑤ |
| MOVE ① | MOVE ② | MOVE ③ | MOVE ④ | MOVE ⑤ |
| MOVE ① | MOVE ② | MOVE ③ | MOVE ④ | MOVE ⑤ |
| MOVE ① | MOVE ② | MOVE ③ | MOVE ④ | MOVE ⑤ |

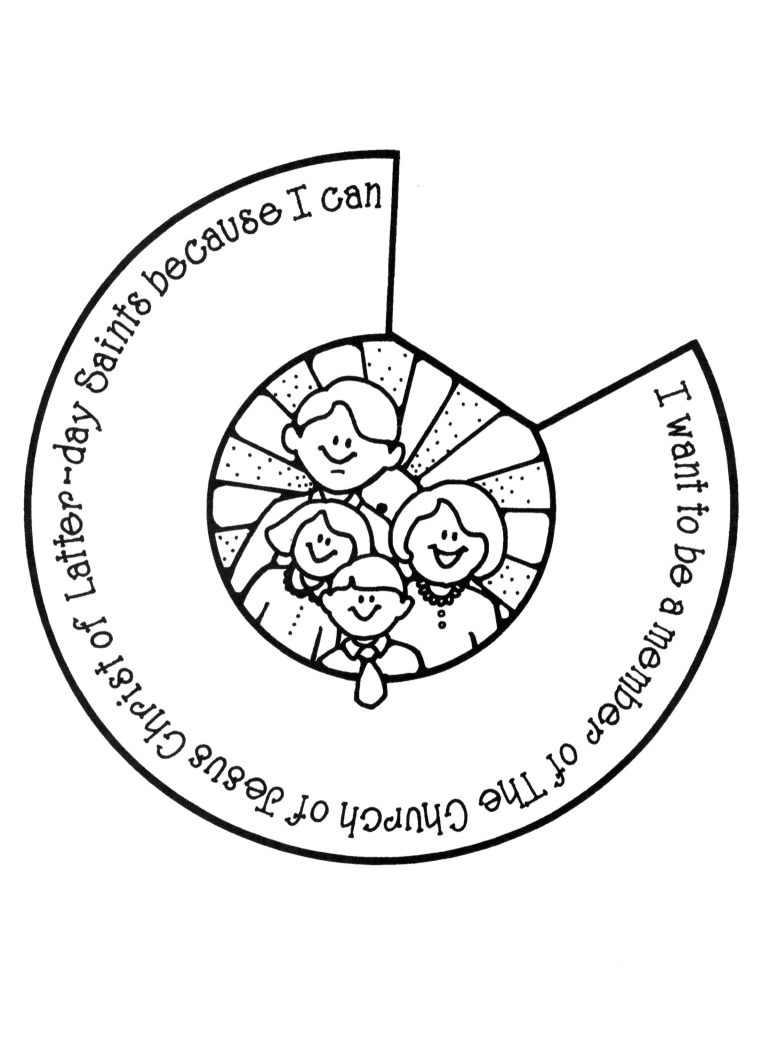

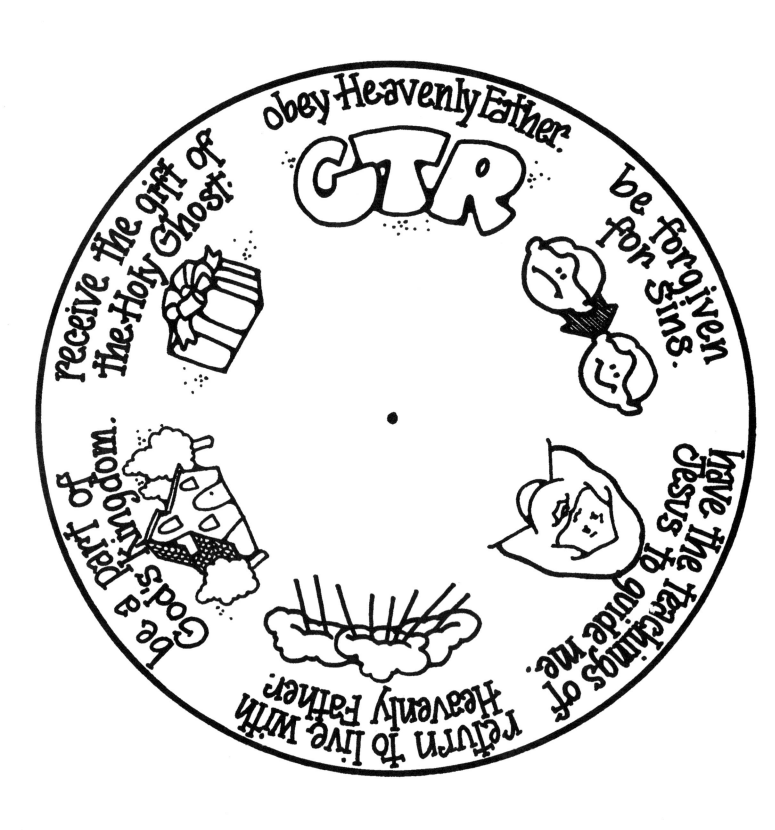

# I PROMISE...

- to obey the commandments
- to read the scriptures
- to honor parents, help others
- to pay tithing
- to attend Primary + sacrament meeting

# Heavenly Father PROMISES...

- to forgive me when I repent
- to love and bless me
- to give me the gift of the Holy Ghost
- to answer my prayers
- to let me live with Him forever

# Theme 3: I Know Who I Am—Psalms 82:6

**SONG:** Sing "I Am a Child of God," *Children's Songbook,* page 2. This song is illustrated in *Primary Partners Singing Fun! I Belong to The Church of Jesus Christ of Latter-day Saints* book and CD-ROM.

Ask: "Do you know who you are, where you came from, what you are blessed with, what spiritual gifts and talents you have, and ways you can serve your family and others?"
Answer the question using the scriptures, Primary lessons, and sources below to teach.

**I Am a Child of God and Lived in Heaven Before I Came to Earth**
(D&C 93:29; 76:24; *Primary 2,* lesson 3).
**I Am a Child of God Blessed with Divine Nature**
(3 Nephi 27:27; *The Family: A Proclamation to the World,* paragraphs 1-2; *Primary 1,* lesson 1).
**I Am a Child of God. He Has Given Me Spiritual Gifts and Talents**
(Article of Faith 7; D&C 46:11; *Primary 5,* lesson 19).

**Sharing Time Activity 1:** I Can Recognize and Seek True Gifts (Gifts of the Spirit Cross Match)

**TO MAKE:** *Copy and color the *Gifts of the Spirit Cross Match* (page 30).
**PREPARATION:** Review Lesson 19 and enrichment activity 1 (page 101) in the *Primary 5 Doctrine and Covenants/Church History Manual.*
**ACTIVITY:** Have children help by drawing a line from the scripture to the gift (of the Spirit) found in the scripture. Talk about the gifts and why it is important to recognize and seek true gifts.

**I Am a Child of God. I Will Serve My Family and Others**
(Mosiah 2:17; *Primary 2,* lesson 39; *Primary 6,* lesson 10, enrichment activities).

**Sharing Time Activity 2:** I Will Use My Talents to Serve Others (Service and Talent Show Poster)

**TO MAKE:** *Copy and color the *Service & Talent Show Poster* (page 31).
**PREPARATION:** Review lesson 26 and enrichment activities 1 and 2 (page 89) in the *Primary 7 New Testament Manual.*
**ACTIVITIES:** This fun ponder poster provides a space for children to write their service goals and draw pictures of themselves performing the service. Help children think of ideas they can write in this *Service and Talent Show Poster.* Examples: Next to the hearts in "The way I treat others" box they might write: "Be kind, listen, smile, be cheerful, or help others." Next to the smiles in "Things I can do" box they might write: "Take out the trash, help clean up, say 'please' or 'thank you,' shine the mirrors, make treats, help with family home evening, read stories to younger brothers or sisters, read scriptures to the family, sing during family home evening."

*All images can be printed in full color or black and white using the CD-ROM:
Primary Partners Teaching Tools—I Belong to The Church of Jesus Christ of Latter-day Saints.

## Sharing Time Activity 3:
I Will Show Love to Others as I Serve
(My Circle of Love Spin-and-Serve Game)

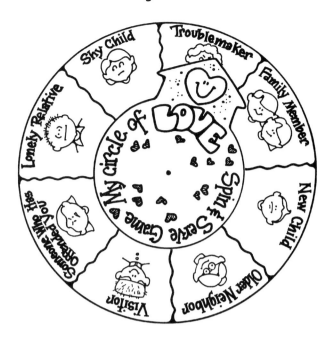

**TO MAKE:** *Copy, color, and cut out the *My Circle of Love Spin-and-Serve Game* (page 32). Attach part A to part B (larger circle) with a metal or button brad. *To make a button brad:* Sew two buttons together on opposite sides (threading thread through the same hole in the paper) to attach wheel parts A and B.

**PREPARATION:** Review lesson 10 and enrichment activities 3 and 4 (pages 41-42) in the *Primary 6 Old Testament Manual.*

**ACTIVITY:** (1) Tell the story how Abraham included Lot and his family in his circle of love. Abraham and Lot divide the land (Genesis 13:1-18). Lot was held captive and rescued by Abraham (Genesis 14:8-16). Abraham asked the Lord to save the righteous people in Sodom and Gomorrah (Genesis 18:16-33). Angels visited Lot in Sodom and he was saved from destruction (Genesis 19:1, 12-17, 24-29). (2) Play *My Circle of Love Spin-and-Serve Game* to talk about ways children can include others in their circle of love. Children spin the center circle, then tell how they will love and serve that person (on the wheel) to include him or her in their circle of love.

## Sharing Time Activity 4: I Can Be Happy as I Serve
(Service Station Sack of Reminders)

**TO MAKE:** *Copy and color the *Service Station Sack of Reminders* label and wordstrips (page 33). Glue label on a brown paper bag. Place wordstrips in the bag.

**PREPARATION:** Review lesson 39 and enrichment activity 3 (page 227) in the *Primary 5 Doctrine and Covenants Manual.*

**ACTIVITY:** Have children take turns pulling out wordstrips. These are acts of kindness we can do to serve others. Talk about the rewards that come from service (e.g. making one feel happy, increasing talents, and the blessings that come from Heavenly Father). If time allows, ask children to share service ideas.

*All images can be printed in full color or black and white using the CD-ROM:
Primary Partners Teaching Tools—I Belong to The Church of Jesus Christ of Latter-day Saints.

# Gifts of the Spirit

Fill in the blank and match the gift with the correct reference.

- Gifts of w_____ and k_____.

- Gift to _____ the testimony of others.

- Gifts of faith to ____ and be _____.

- Gift of p_____.

- Gift to ____ that Jesus is the _____.

- Gift to s____ and understand languages.

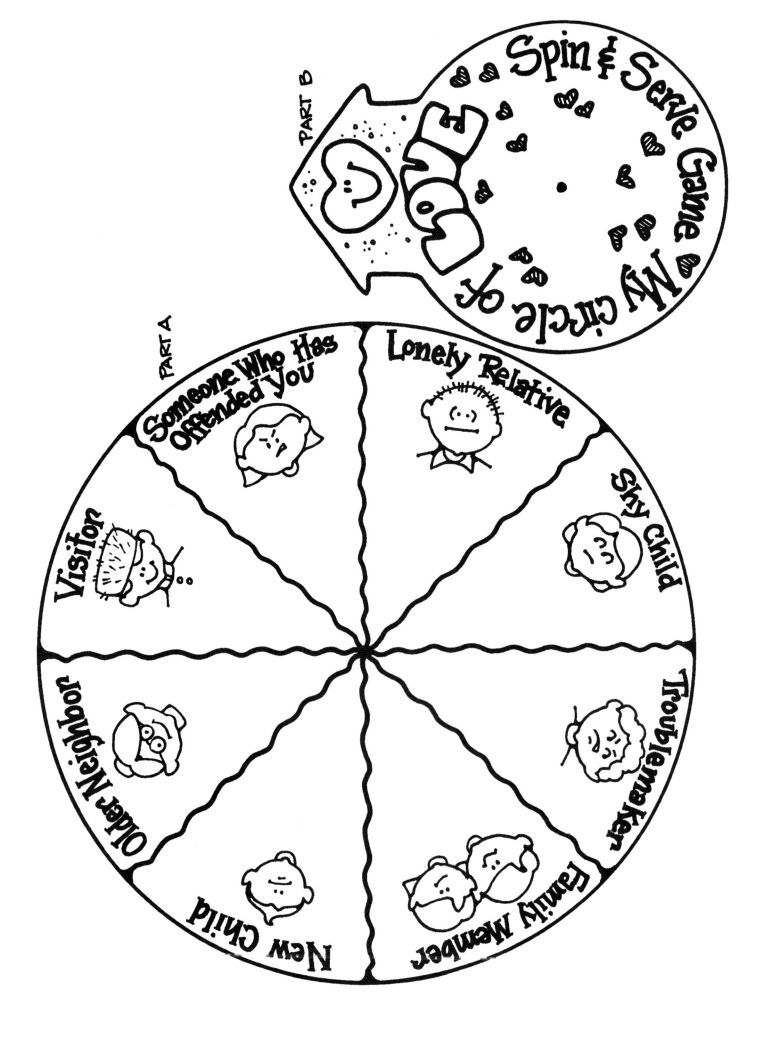

You're at the SERVICE STATION! Gas up, take off and help those you car about.

| | |
|---|---|
| Read a story to sister or brother. | Rake leaves, but not in trees. |
| Make someone's bed. | Do housework without a shirk. |
| Fix a snack and deliver. | Fix breakfast for mom or dad. |
| Vacuum with vigor 10 minutes. | Ask your family how you can help. |
| Wipe mirrors with window cleaner. | Dust your best to pass the white glove test. |
| Set the table for Aunt Mabel. | Pick out a recipe and cook up a storm (great food)! |
| Visit and cheer up the elderly. | Make a vegetable snack for dinner. |
| Write a love note and deliver. | Compliment someone by saying "cool ____," or "great ____." |
| Make your own snack and clean up the dishes. | Take a treat to someone on your street. |
| Be a dirt detective (sweep the floor). | Wash and wipe the dishes. |

… Theme 4 — I Belong to The Church

# Theme 4: I Believe in the Savior, Jesus Christ—Matthew 16:16

**SONG:** Sing "Easter Hosanna," *Children's Songbook*, page 68. This song is illustrated in *Primary Partners Singing Fun! I Belong to The Church of Jesus Christ of Latter-day Saints* book and CD-ROM.

Ask: "Do you know who the Savior Jesus Christ is and have faith in Him?"
Answer the question using the scriptures, Primary lessons, and sources below to teach.

> **Jesus Is the Savior of All Mankind. I Have Faith in the Lord Jesus Christ**
> (Article of Faith 4; Mosiah 3:9; *Primary 4*, lesson 43).

## Sharing Time Activity 1: Jesus Suffered for Me (Atonement Ponder Wheel)

**TO MAKE:** *Copy, color, and cut out the *Atonement Ponder Wheel* (pages 37-38). Cut out the window on part A with scissors or a razor blade. Place a paper fastener (metal brad) in the center to turn the wheel.

**PREPARATION:** Review lesson 32 and the enrichment activity 1 (page 111) in the *Primary 7 New Testament Manual*.

**ACTIVITY:** With this wheel you can show children what Jesus said while hanging on the cross. These statements tell of the power and character of Jesus that helped Him to say and do these things. Have children take turns reading and discuss the statements Jesus made, e.g., Luke 23:34 says that Jesus was "merciful and forgiving."

*All images can be printed in full color or black and white using the CD-ROM: Primary Partners Teaching Tools—I Belong to The Church of Jesus Christ of Latter-day Saints.*

**As I Have Faith, I Want to Repent and Be Baptized**
(Mosiah 18:10; *Primary 2*, lesson 12; *Primary 4*, lesson 14).

## Sharing Time Activity 2: I Can Live in Heaven (Alma the Younger's Road to Repentance Maze)

**TO MAKE:** *Copy and color the *Alma the Younger's Road to Repentance Maze* (page 39). If doing two sharing times, make an additional copy as children will be drawing through the maze.

**PREPARATION:** Review lesson 14 and the scripture account (pages 47-48) in the *Primary 4 Book of Mormon Manual*.

**ACTIVITY:** Help children get through the maze, reminding them that repentance is necessary for earthly happiness and eternal life.

*How to Get Through Maze:* Alma the Younger chose the wrong path. Help him get back on. Read the choice and choose for yourself the direction to go in order to repent and choose the righteous path.

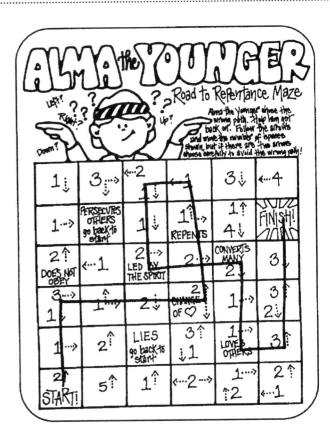

## Sharing Time Activity 3: Jesus Helped Me Overcome Sin and Death (Repentance Puzzle)

**TO MAKE:** *Copy and color the *Repentance Puzzle* (page 40). If doing two sharing times, make an additional copy as children will be writing on the puzzle.

**PREPARATION:** Review lesson 30 and the enrichment activity 3 (page 104) in the *Primary 7 New Testament Manual*.

**ACTIVITY:** Read Mosiah 14:35 and Alma 7:11-12. Tell children that when Jesus suffered in the Garden of Gethsemane, He helped us overcome sin by suffering for our sins. This makes it possible for us to repent and be forgiven. He also suffered death, which makes it possible for us to live again. Fill in the puzzle using the words in the statement below.

*All images can be printed in full color or black and white using the CD-ROM: Primary Partners Teaching Tools—I Belong to The Church of Jesus Christ of Latter-day Saints.*

**I Will Receive the Gift of the Holy Ghost** (2 Nephi 32:5; *Primary 1*, lesson 7; *Primary 2*, lesson 13).

**Sharing Time Activity 4:** The Holy Ghost Will Guide and Comfort Me (Invite the Spirit Choice Game)

**TO MAKE:** *Copy, color, and cut out the *Invite the Spirit Choice Game* (pages 41-42). Place wordstrips in a container or bag to draw from. Cut the label in the center and post the "Invites the Spirit" and the "Turns the Spirit Away" labels on the board or a poster. *Option:* Tape the wordstrips on the sides and bottom on the top and bottom of a poster, leaving the top open to insert wordstrips while playing the game.
*Note:* If making individual games for children, fold label and place label and wordstrips in a zip-close plastic bag (shown right).

**PREPARATION:** Review lesson 7 and enrichment activity 5 (page 34) in the *Primary 5 Doctrine and Covenants/Church History Manual*.

**ACTIVITY:** Children can learn about choices that invite the Spirit of the Holy Ghost and those that turn it away.
*To Play:* Divide children into two teams. Take turns drawing a choice wordstrip from the bag and reading it aloud. The player makes a choice by saying, "Invites the Spirit," or "Turns the Spirit Away." Each right choice is 1 point. Tape the wordstrips below the label placed on the board or poster. Play 10-15 minutes or until all wordstrips are read. *Option:* Place wordstrips in pockets (see details above).

**As I Choose the Right Each Day, I Can Return to Heavenly Father**
(D&C 6:13; *Primary 2*, lesson 14; *Primary 3*, lesson 3).

**Sharing Time Activity 5:**
Happiness Comes from Choosing the Right (CTR Happiness Wheel)

**TO MAKE:** *Copy, color, and cut out the *CTR Happiness Wheel* parts A and B (pages 43-44) Place a paper fastener (metal brad) in the center to attach wheels.

**PREPARATION:** Review lesson 1 and the teacher presentation (page 2) in the *Primary 2-CTR A Manual*.

**ACTIVITY:** Show children the *CTR Happiness Wheel* to help them learn how happiness can come from choosing the right. As children take turns spinning the wheel, talk about ways they can choose the right and how these choices can help them to be happy. Tell them that each of these ways can prepare them to enter the temple.

*All images can be printed in full color or black and white using the CD-ROM:
*Primary Partners Teaching Tools—I Belong to The Church of Jesus Christ of Latter-day Saints*.

# The Seven Sayings of Christ on the Cross

**Outer ring (clockwise from top):**
- Concern for Mother
- Needed Heavenly Father
- Did His Father's Will
- Fulfilled the plan
- Merciful and forgiving
- Knew the future

**Inner ring (references):**
- John 19:26-27
- Matt. 27:46
- Luke 23:46
- Matt. 27:50
- Luke 23:34
- Luke 23:43

# ALMA the YOUNGER
## Road to Repentance Maze

Left? Right? Down? Up?

Alma the Younger chose the wrong path. Help him get back on. Follow the arrows and move the number of spaces shown, but if there are two arrows choose carefully to avoid the wrong path!

| | | | | | |
|---|---|---|---|---|---|
| 1 ↓ | 3 ⋯→ ↓ | ←⋯2 / 1 ↓ | ←⋯1 | 3 ↓ | ←⋯4 |
| 1 ⋯→ | PERSECUTES OTHERS go back to start | 1 ↓ | 1 ↑ ⋯→ REPENTS | 1 ↑ / 4 ↓ | FINISH! |
| 2 ↑ DOES NOT OBEY | ←⋯1 | 2 ⋯→ LED BY THE SPIRIT | 2 ⋯→ | CONVERTS MANY 2 ↓ | 3 ↓ |
| 3 ⋯→ / 1 ↓ | 1 ↑ ⋯→ | 2 ↓ | CHANGE OF ♡ 2 ↑ ↓ | 1 ⋯→ | 3 ↑ / 2 ↓ |
| 1 ⋯→ | 2 ↑ | LIES go back to start | 3 ↑ / ↓ 1 | 1 ⋯→ LOVES OTHERS | 3 ↑ |
| 2 ↑ START! | 5 ↑ | 1 ↑ | ←⋯2⋯→ | 1 ⋯→ / ↑ 2 | 2 ↑ / ←⋯1 |

| | |
|---|---|
| search the scriptures for truth | pray with real intent |
| get even when you feel hurt | be forgiving and kind |
| feel happy when others are sad | take something without asking |
| volunteer and help older person | thank teacher for lesson |
| be reverent in church | pay tithing on all money earned |
| take a toy away from brother | take something without paying |
| help brother or sister | wash dishes without being asked |
| watch a scary movie | tease younger sister |
| frighten someone | tell the untruth |
| miss family home evening | have family prayer |
| set the table for dinner | take out garbage |
| skip doing homework | talk bad about teacher |
| sass mother | talk rude about a friend |
| frown all day | forgive someone |
| go to bed late | go to be early and get up early |
| keep a record of your people by writing in your journal | tried to keep the Sabbath holy |
| told a friend you'd call but didn't | your plant died from neglect |
| spend your tithing money | don't obey all the commandments |
| trust in others rather than Jesus | waste someone's time |
| don't help when needed | don't listen |
| care for others more than self | can't wait to read standard works |
| take more food than you can eat | eat too much food |
| skipped serving a mission | married outside temple |
| told a dirty joke | saw someone steal and not tell |
| talked during a lesson at church | borrowed a pen and didn't return |
| asked a friend to come to church | helped a friend in need |
| asked your mother if you could help | made your brother's bed |
| write a thank you note to teacher | cheered up the sad |
| went home sick when you felt good | didn't go straight home or call |

Part A

Part A

Part B

# Theme 5: The Prophet Speaks for the Savior. I Can Follow the Prophet Today—D&C 1:38

**SONG:** Sing "The Things I Do," *Children's Songbook*, page 170. This song is illustrated in *Primary Partners Singing Fun! I Belong to The Church of Jesus Christ of Latter-day Saints* book and CD-ROM.

Ask: "How can the prophet today speak for the Savior? How can we follow the prophet's teachings today? What are some things the prophet has said that we can share with our family?" Answer the questions using the scriptures, Primary lessons, and sources below to teach.

---
**A Prophet Is a Man Called by Our Father in Heaven to Speak for Him**
(Exodus 3:1-6, 9-12; 1 Samuel 3:1-10, 19-20; Moses 6:26-39; Joseph Smith—History 1:11-20; *Primary 1*, lesson 43; *Gospel Principles*, chapter 9.
---

## Sharing Time Activity 1:
### I Know the Prophet Lives
(Prophet Poster Fold-out Pictures)

**TO MAKE:** *Copy, color, and cut out the *Prophet Poster Fold-out Pictures* (page 49). Tape or glue part B to the bottom of part A where indicated. Fold on middle line and fan-fold. Or, cut individual pictures out to display.

**PREPARATION:** Review lesson 43 (pages 142-143) in the *Primary 1—Nursery and Age 3 Manual*.

**ACTIVITY:** Show children pictures of prophets who talk to Heavenly Father and Jesus. Talk about each, e.g., Moses, Joseph Smith, and the current prophet today (drawing in his face). Let children know they are blessed when they follow the prophet.

*All images can be printed in full color or black and white using the CD-ROM: Primary Partners Teaching Tools—I Belong to The Church of Jesus Christ of Latter-day Saints.

Primary Partners Teaching Tools — I Belong to The Church — Theme 5

**Sharing Time Activity 2:**
**I Will Listen to the Prophet to Stay in the Light (Cycle of History Wheel)**

**TO MAKE:** *Copy, color, and cut out the *Cycle of History Wheel* (pages 50-51). Attach part A on top of part B with a metal or button brad (placed in the center). *To make button brad:* Sew two buttons together on opposite sides (threading thread through the same hole in the paper) to attach wheel parts A and B. To use wheel see page 56 (the pattern page) for details.

**PREPARATION:** Review lesson 41 and the enrichment activity 3 (page 146) in the *Primary 4 Book of Mormon Manual.*

**ACTIVITY:** Create a *Cycle of History Wheel* that children can turn as you share stories of times in the scriptures when people listened to and followed the prophet and times when they did not (detailed on the following page). The *Primary 4 Book of Mormon Manual* (page 146) enrichment activity suggests you make wordstrips with the words, e.g., righteous, blessings, prosperity, pride, wickedness, suffering or destruction, humility, and repentance (shown on the cycle of history above). Use the wheel, instead of the wordstrips to:
1. Explain that throughout history when people have been righteous, Heavenly Father has blessed them with prosperity. Unfortunately this prosperity can lead to pride and wickedness and sometimes complete destruction.
2. Explain to children what happened to the Jaredites, who were righteous and blessed, and prospered. Turn the arrow to "Righteous," "Blessing," and "Prosperity" (as shown above).
3. Explain that the Jaredites then became proud and rejected the prophets. The people became so wicked that they were entirely destroyed. Turn the arrow to "Pride," "Wickedness," and "Suffering and Destruction."
4. Explain that if the Jaredites had humbled themselves and repented before they were destroyed, they could have returned to enjoying the blessings of righteous living. Turn the arrow to "Humility" and "Repent."
5. Explain that this cycle often happens in our personal lives as well as in the history of nations.
6. Go through *Cycle of History Wheel* again starting with "Humility" and talk about each action and where it leads.

*All images can be printed in full color or black and white using the CD-ROM:
Primary Partners Teaching Tools—I Belong to The Church of Jesus Christ of Latter-day Saints.

**The Living Prophet Is a Special Witness of Jesus Christ.
He Bears Testimony of Heavenly Father and Jesus Christ**
(D&C 27:12; 1 Nephi 10:5; Jacob 7:11).

## Sharing Time Activity 3: The Prophet Speaks and I Listen (Revelation Routes)

**TO MAKE:** *Copy and color the *Revelation Routes* (page 52).

**PREPARATION:** Review lesson 15 and discussion and application question 4 (page 78) in the *Primary 5 Doctrine and Covenants/Church History Manual.*

**ACTIVITY:** Have children draw an arrow to whoever receives revelation for whom (e.g., the prophet receives revelation for the whole Church so draw a line from the prophet to everyone except Heavenly Father and Jesus Christ).

## Sharing Time Activity 4: Prophets Tell Me about the Life and Mission of Jesus (Prophet Presentation)

**TO MAKE:** *Copy, color, and cut out the *Prophet Poster Presentation* (pages 53-54). Glue the matching cue card to back of poster.

**PREPARATION:** Review lesson 31 and the attention activity and scripture account and discussion (pages 111-112) in the *Primary 4 Book of Mormon Manual.*

**ACTIVITIES:** Help children learn about the Prophets Alma, Samuel the Lamanite, Nephi, and Abinadi who told the people of the life and mission of Jesus Christ. Show the poster and read the matching cue card. Present the activity in one of the following ways (detailed on page 48):

*All images can be printed in full color or black and white using the CD-ROM:
*Primary Partners Teaching Tools—I Belong to The Church of Jesus Christ of Latter-day Saints.*

*Activity 1: Prophet Show-and-Tell:*

1. Post the four prophets on the board or a poster.
2. Ask children to guess the prophet as you read about each, omitting their name as you read. After they guess, write their names below their pictures.
3. Talk about the prophets again, asking children to tell you what they know about each prophet. Be prepared to tell them something more that you know about each prophet.

*Activity 2: Guess the Prophet Scripture Search:*

1. Ahead of time find scriptures about the prophets: Alma, Samuel the Lamanite, Nephi, and Abinadi. These could be scriptures about things they said or did. Write out the scriptures and the references on slips of paper and place them in a container.
2. Post the four prophets on the board with names below.
3. Have children take turns drawing scriptures from the container, reading them aloud and guessing the prophet. If they don't guess correctly, they can search the scriptures to find the answer. Play in teams, and have them race to find the answers.

---

**The Testimony of the Prophet Strengthens My Faith in Jesus Christ
and Guides Us in These Latter-days**
(Jacob 4:4-5; D&C 76:19-23; examples from conference talks in the *Friend*, *Ensign*, and *Liahona*).

---

## Sharing Time Activity 5:
### The Prophets Give Latter-day Revelation (Standard Works Think-athon)

**TO MAKE:** *Copy, color, and cut out the *Standard Works Think-athon* block, quiz wordstrips, and rules (pages 55-57). Fold box and glue tabs inside. Place wordstrips inside a container to draw from.

**PREPARATION:** Review lesson 22 and enrichment activity 1 (page 118) in the *Primary 5 Doctrine and Covenants/Church History Manual*.

**ACTIVITY:** This *Standard Works Think-athon* game will help children become more familiar with the standard works, which contain the words of the prophets. Follow the rules (page 57). Before playing talk about the standard works, telling children that the prophets of each time period told about Jesus Christ. Read and talk about each wordstrip and then have a quiz by playing the game.

*All images can be printed in full color or black and white using the CD-ROM:
Primary Partners Teaching Tools—I Belong to The Church of Jesus Christ of Latter-day Saints.

**TO USE WHEEL:**
• Read the scriptures shown right.
• Turn the arrow to the place in time found in the scripture. Notice if the people were in the light or the dark cycle in history.
• The prophets warn us to think about our own lives and where we are in the cycle of history. Ask yourself: What can I do to turn toward the light?

**SCRIPTURES:**
4 Nephi 1:18
Alma 7:17
Ether 10:28
Alma 4:12
1 Nephi 7:20
3 Nephi 10:18
Helaman 3:25-26
Ether 6:12
Helaman 6:1
Enos 1:4-5
Alma 4:1-3
3 Nephi 2:3
4 Nephi 1:24
Helaman 4:15
Alma 8:14
3 Nephi 8:25
Alma 48:20
Helaman 12:1

**TO USE WHEEL:**
• Read the scriptures shown right.
• Turn the arrow to the place in time found in the scripture. Notice if the people were in the light or the dark cycle in history.
• The prophets warn us to think about our own lives and where we are in the cycle of history. Ask yourself: What can I do to turn toward the light?

**SCRIPTURES:**
4 Nephi 1:18
Alma 7:17
Ether 10:28
Alma 4:12
1 Nephi 7:20
3 Nephi 10:18
Helaman 3:25-26
Ether 6:12
Helaman 6:1
Enos 1:4-5
Alma 4:1-3
3 Nephi 2:3
4 Nephi 1:24
Helaman 4:15
Alma 8:14
3 Nephi 8:25
Alma 48:20
Helaman 12:1

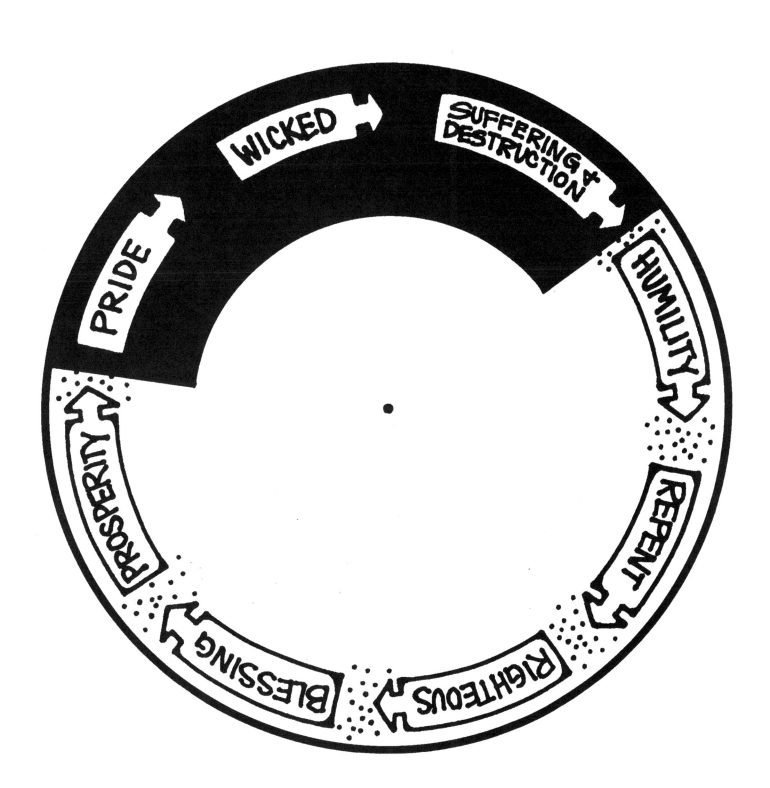

The Nephite Prophet **Alma** had a vision of Jesus about 100 years before He was born. He saw that Jesus would be born of Mary in Jerusalem. He would suffer pains and afflictions and temptations of every kind that we might be saved. He would loose the bands of death for everyone. - Alma 7:10-12

**Samuel the Lamanite** Prophet stood on a city wall and told the people that Jesus would be born in five years. He said a sign would come—great lights would be in heaven. And in the night before He was born there would be no darkness; it would be like day. The day of His birth a new star would appear.
- Helaman 14:2-6

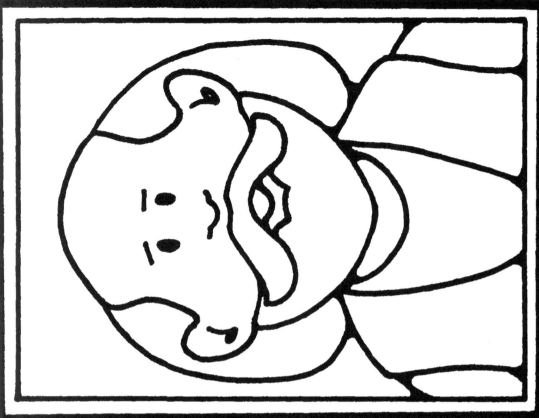

The Prophet **Abinadi** lived 150 years before Jesus. Abinadi told the people that "God himself shall come down among the children of men, and shall redeem His people . . . (breaking) the bands of death, (taking) upon himself their iniquity (sins). . . ."
- Mosiah 15:1; 7-9

The Prophet **Nephi** the son of Lehi lived 600 years before Jesus. He told of his vision, seeing the virgin, the mother of the Son of God, bearing a child in her arms.    - Nephi 11:20-22

## STANDARD WORKS THINK-ATHON RULES:

1. Divide players into two teams. Have one team member at a time represent each team.
2. Teams take turns answering the question.
3. Leader draws a wordstrip and reads the think-athon question.
4. Each team has 10 seconds to answer the question by guessing Book of Mormon, Pearl of Great Price, Doctrine and Covenants, or the Bible, or the question will be given to the other team.
5. When team members answer question correctly, they may roll the die to win points for their team. The roll of the die must match the answer to the question to receive 1 point for their team. For example, if the answer is Bible, they must roll Bible. If they roll "bonus," they receive 2 points. If they roll "roll again," they get another chance to win a point.
6. The team with the most points wins!

## STANDARD WORKS THINK-ATHON RULES:

1. Divide players into two teams. Have one team member at a time represent each team.
2. Teams take turns answering the question.
3. Leader draws a wordstrip and reads the think-athon question.
4. Each team has 10 seconds to answer the question by guessing Book of Mormon, Pearl of Great Price, Doctrine and Covenants, or the Bible, or the question will be given to the other team.
5. When team members answer question correctly, they may roll the die to win points for their team. The roll of the die must match the answer to the question to receive 1 point for their team. For example, if the answer is Bible, they must roll Bible. If they roll "bonus," they receive 2 points. If they roll "roll again," they get another chance to win a point.
6. The team with the most points wins!

| | |
|---|---|
| Which book tells us about the prophecies of Jesus Christ?    Answer: Bible and Book of Mormon | Which book contains the sacrament prayers?    Answer: Doctrine & Covenants and Book of Mormon |
| Which book tells about the Savior's life and teachings when he was on the earth?    Answer: Bible | Which book tells of the restoration of the Aaronic Priesthood by John the Baptist?    Answer: D&C |
| Which book is another testament of Jesus Christ?    Answer: Book of Mormon | Which book tells of qualities of a missionary?    Answer: Doctrine and Covenants |
| Which book tells about the Savior's dealings with the people in the American continent?    Answer: Book of Mormon | Which book tells of the prophet receiving revelation for the whole Church?    Answer: Doctrine and Covenants |
| Which book is a collection of revelations from Jesus Christ for the latter days, or our times?    Answer: Doctrine and Covenants | Which book tells these stories: Jonah and the whale, David and Goliath, and Shadrach, Meshach, and Abed-nego?    Answer: Bible |
| Which book gives us teachings and testimonies of Jesus Christ from ancient prophets as well as Joseph Smith's history and testimony of Heavenly Father and Jesus Christ?    Answer: Pearl of Great Price | Which book tells the stories of Adam and Eve, Noah and the ark, Joseph sold into Egypt, the ten commandments, and Queen Ester?    Answer: Bible |
| Which book tells more about the Lord and His people in the Holy Land, beginning with the earth's creation?    Answer: Bible | Which book told the stories of Alma the Younger and Amulek, peace in America, and crossing the sea to the promised land?    Answer: Book of Mormon |
| Which book tells of Jesus Christ visiting the people on the American continent?    Answer: Book of Mormon | Which book tells of Enos, King Benjamin, Abinadi and King Noah, Helaman and the 2,000 young men?    Answer: Book of Mormon |
| Which book tells the most about the birth of Jesus and His life on earth?    Answer: Bible | Which book tells of the three kingdoms of heaven?    Answer: Doctrine and Covenants |
| Which book is a record of Heavenly Father and Jesus Christ appearing to Joseph Smith in the Sacred Grove?    Answer: Pearl of Great Price | Which book contains Joseph Smith's translations of the book of Matthew (from the Bible)?    Answer: Pearl of Great Price |
| All of the standard works testify of Jesus Christ. Which one testifies of Jesus Christ visiting people in Ancient America?    Answer: Book of Mormon | Which book contains translations from the ancient writings of Abraham? These records were found in the catacombs of Egypt.    Answer: Pearl of Great Price |
| Which book tells how the Church should be established in the last days?    Answer: Doctrine and Covenants | Which book contains the Book of Moses (parts of the Bible) translated by Joseph Smith?    Answer: Pearl of Great Price |
| Which book tells about the Word of Wisdom?    Answer: Doctrine and Covenants | Which book contains the Articles of Faith?    Answer: Pearl of Great Price |

# Theme 6: I Know God's Plan—Moses 1:39

**SONG:** Sing "I Lived in Heaven," *Children's Songbook,* page 4. This song is illustrated in *Primary Partners Singing Fun! I Belong to The Church of Jesus Christ of Latter-day Saints* book and CD-ROM.

Ask: "What is Heavenly Father's plan for us?"
Answer the question using the scriptures, Primary lessons, and sources below to teach.

---

**Jesus Is My Savior. Because of Him I Can Have Eternal Life**
(Article of Faith 3; *Primary 4*, lesson 45; *Primary 6*, lesson 45).

---

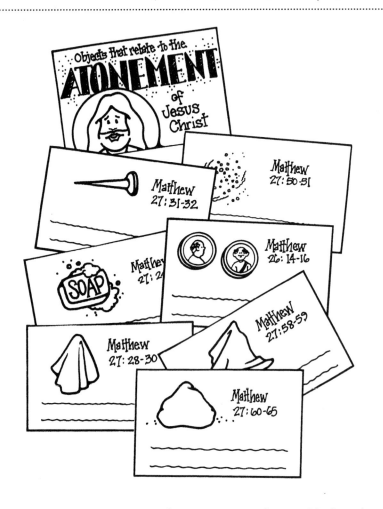

**Sharing Time Activity 1:** Jesus Gave Me Immortality and Eternal Life (Atonement Object Lesson)

**TO MAKE:** *Copy, color, and cut out the *Atonement Object Lesson* cards (page 63).

**PREPARATION:** Review lesson 45 and the enrichment activity 6 (pages 205-206) in the *Primary 6 Old Testament Manual.*

**ACTIVITY:** Place real objects with Atonement object cards attached or just the object cards in a basket or sack. Ask children to take turns drawing an object card and reading the scripture on the card. Ask them to tell the meaning of the scripture and how it relates to the object. Have children take turns reading the scripture and writing the meaning on the card below the scripture. Example: on the coins card—Matthew 26:14-16 they could write: "Jesus was betrayed for 30 pieces of silver." Ask children to color one cloth red—*"scarlet"* (Matthew 27:28-30) and leave the other cloth white—*"clean linen"* (Matthew 27:58-59).

*All images can be printed in full color or black and white using the CD-ROM:
*Primary Partners Teaching Tools—I Belong to The Church of Jesus Christ of Latter-day Saints.*

**Heavenly Father and Jesus Created the Earth and All Forms of Life.
I Can Treat the Earth and All Living Things with Respect** (3 Nephi 9:15; *Primary 6*, lessons 1, 3).

### Sharing Time Activity 2:
### Heavenly Father's Plan Is for Me
### (Plan of Salvation Storyboard and Quiz)

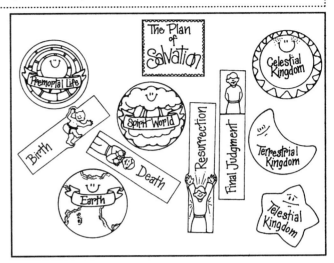

**TO MAKE:** *Copy, color, and cut out the *Plan of Salvation Storyboard and Quiz* and wordstrips (pages 64-65).
**PREPARATION:** Review less. 1 and the enrichment activities 3, 5, and 6 (p. 4) in *Primary 6 Old Test. Manual*.
**ACTIVITIES:**
**Idea 1:** Create a *Plan of Salvation Storyboard*. Place the storyboard figures on the wall with tape as you discuss the questions on pages 2-3 in the Primary 6 manual.
**Idea 2:** Premortal Life and Earth Life Quiz. Place quiz wordstrips (e.g. "Life with Heavenly Father and Jesus") facedown. Children can draw a quiz wordstrip and place it on the storyboard under premortal life, earth or both. *Answers:* Live with Heavenly Father and Jesus Christ (premortal), Be with our family (earth), Have the Bible and Book of Mormon to guide us (earth), Have only a spirit body (premortal), Have a physical body (earth), Be taught Heavenly Father's plan (both), Experience hard work, sorrow, and death (earth), and Be able to have children (earth). Encourage children to present quiz to family and friends.

**Agency Is a Gift from Heavenly Father. As I Choose Between Right and Wrong, I Am Accountable**
(Articles of Faith 1:2; Alma 34:32; *Primary 2*, lesson 5).

### Sharing Time Activity 3:
### Heavenly Father Trusts Us to Follow (Heaven Road Map)

**TO MAKE:** *Copy, color, and cut out the *Heaven Road Map* and trusty truck (page 66).
**PREPARATION:** Review lesson 2 and the game (page 73) in the *Primary 3— CTR B Manual*.
**ACTIVITY:** (1) Divide children into two teams and give each a trusty truck to place on the start position. (2) Tell children that when they are on the road of life, if they make "trusty" decisions they are living Heavenly Father's plan, and they get closer to heaven. If they don't make "trusty" decisions, they end up on the DEAD END path, which does not allow them to progress or gain happiness.
(3) Have each team take turns moving along the path with their trusty truck. Wherever they stop, have them make up a situation and tell the decision they will make that will make them trustworthy. Keep going around the map until the time is up (about 15 minutes).
*Note:* You may want to have situations written ahead of time for each stop: School, CTR Circle, Church, Dead End, and Don't Forget to Pray Park. When children can't think of a situation, they can draw a card for that map location. Write the map location on the back of each card and place cards in piles to find quickly. For example, when children land on CTR Circle, they draw a card labeled "CTR Circle" on the back.

*All images can be printed in full color or black and white using the CD-ROM:
Primary Partners Teaching Tools—I Belong to The Church of Jesus Christ of Latter-day Saints.*

## Sharing Time Activity 4: Heavenly Father Gave Me Free Agency (Choices Slap Game)

**TO MAKE:** *Copy, color, and cut out the *Choices Slap Game* pad and game rules (pages 67-68).

**PREPARATION:** Review lesson 5 and the activity/summary (page 23) in the *Primary 2-CTR A Manual*.

**ACTIVITY:** Help children learn how to make choices by slapping the frowning faces or the smiling faces slap pad when a choice is given to them. Divide children into two teams and have a child from each team come up to the board where the slap pad is posted. At the word "go," the leader reads an action (found on page 75, or add other actions to activity). The two teams race to slap the pad. The first team to slap the right answer wins a point for their team. Read the choices following the game rules on p. 75.

## Sharing Time Activity 5: I Will Show Heavenly Father and Jesus Respect (Respectful Choices Poster)

**TO MAKE:** *Copy, color, and cut out the *I Can Show Respect Poster* and pictures (pages 69-70).

**PREPARATION:** Review lesson 8 and the attention activity (page 25) in the *Primary 7 New Testament Manual*.

**ACTIVITY:**
Encourage children to show respect to others by matching and taping on the pictures with the "RESPECT" and "DISRESPECT" categories on the chart. Discuss why respectful choices please Heavenly Father and Jesus.

*All images can be printed in full color or black and white using the CD-ROM: Primary Partners Teaching Tools—I Belong to The Church of Jesus Christ of Latter-day Saints.

# I Have Been Sent to a Family to Learn to Follow Jesus
(1 Nephi 1:1; *Primary 2*, lesson 6; *Primary 3*, lesson 28).

## Sharing Time Activity 6: My Testimony of Jesus
(What Would Jesus Do? Choice Situation Sack)

**TO MAKE:** *Copy, color, and cut out the *What Would Jesus Do? Choice Situation Sack* label and cards (page 71).
*Note:* This activity can also be used for Theme 8, activity 1 (page 87).

**PREPARATION:** Review lesson 8 and enrichment activity 1 in the *Primary 4 Book of Mormon Manual*.

**ACTIVITY:** Tell children they can be worthy of the blessings of the temple as they follow Jesus. Give each child a mint and say, "Jesus 'mint' for us to be happy, to come to the temple, which is God's house, and share in the blessings there. To be able to go to the temple someday, we must follow Jesus, walk in His steps, and do what He would do and say." Have children reach into the sack, draw out a situation, read it, and then tell what Jesus would do.

## Sharing Time Activity 7:
I Will Live the Gospel of Jesus Christ
(Faithful Footsteps Goal Flip Chart)

**TO MAKE:** *Copy, color, and cut out the *Faithful Footsteps Goal Flip Chart* (pages 72-74).

**PREPARATION:** Review Lesson 6 and the enrichment activity 7 (page 26) in the *Primary 6 Old Testament Manual*.

**ACTIVITY:** Help children follow in the footsteps of Jesus as they endure to the end.
1. Post chart on the board or poster.
2. Help children write things they can do on each chart to keep that commandment.
3. Tell them that each step brings them closer to eternal life, to live with Heavenly Father and Jesus.
4. Read 2 Nephi 31:20. "Press forward" means to walk in the steps of Jesus, to do as He would do. As we "press forward," enduring to the end, we shall have the greatest of all gifts, eternal life (and live with Heavenly Father and Jesus).

*All images can be printed in full color or black and white using the CD-ROM:
*Primary Partners Teaching Tools—I Belong to The Church of Jesus Christ of Latter-day Saints*.

### Sharing Time Activity 8:
*Jesus Christ Was Chosen to Be My Savior (Choices & Consequences Match Game)*

**TO MAKE:** *Copy, color, and cut out the *Choices & Consequences Match Game* (pages 75-76).

**PREPARATION:** Review lesson 2 and enrichment activity 2 (page 7) in the *Primary 6 Old Testament Manual*.

**ACTIVITY:** Play the *Choice & Consequences Match Game* to show what can happen when we make good and bad choices. (1) Turn cards over and place facedown, randomly on the left of the board or poster. (2) Divide children into two teams. (3) Take turns turning over two cards to make a match. When a match is made, tape it to the right of the board or poster. Notice the pointed cards are the choices and the indented cards are the consequences (making it easier to match).

### Sharing Time Activity 9:
*I Can Be like Jesus (Compassion Wheel)*

**TO MAKE:** *Copy, color, and cut out the *Compassion Wheel* (pages 77-78). Attach part A on top of part B with a metal or button brad in the center. *To make a button brad:* Sew two buttons together on opposite sides (threading thread through the same hole in the papers) to attach compassion wheels.

**PREPARATION:** Review lesson 13 and enrichment activity 2 (page 46) in *Primary 7 New Testament Manual*.

**ACTIVITY:** Read 1 John 3:18 and help children learn how to show love and compassion as Jesus did when He healed the sick. Use the *Compassion Wheel* to show them things they can do to show love. Have children look at the blank circle and imagine what they would be doing to show love and compassion. If giving the children a wheel to take home, ask them to draw a picture of something they did or can do to show love and compassion in each of the circles.

*All images can be printed in full color or black and white using the CD-ROM: Primary Partners Teaching Tools—I Belong to The Church of Jesus Christ of Latter-day Saints.*

# The Plan of Salvation

**Birth**
- Have a physical body
- Learn about Heavenly Father's plan
- Experience hard work, sorrow, and death
- Be able to have children

**Death**
- Live with Heavenly Father and Jesus
- Be with our family
- Have the scriptures to guide us
- Have only a spirit body

**Resurrection**

**Final Judgment**

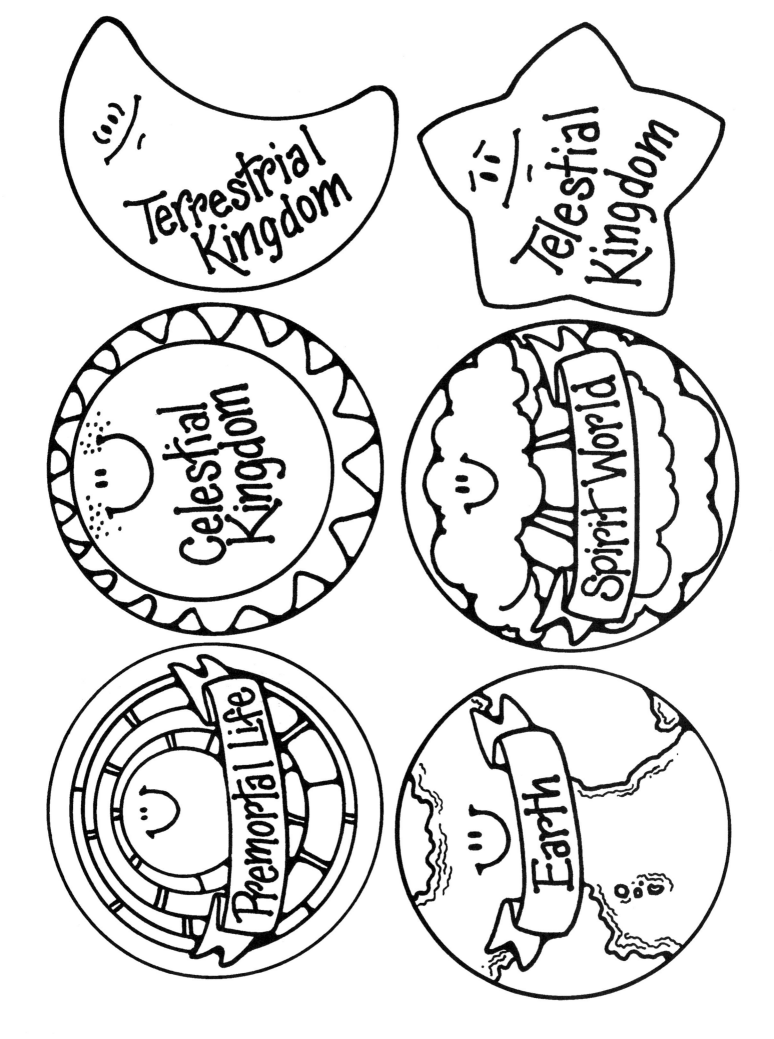

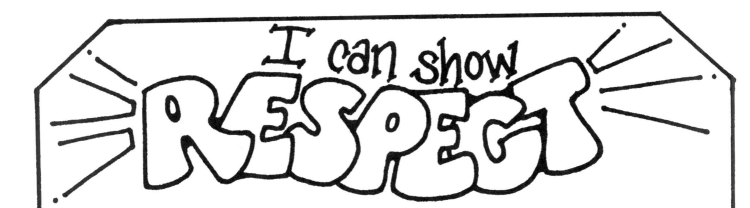

| When someone asks me to steal, I say, "No deal!" | When asked to taste beer or wine, I decline. | When temptation is near, I choose the right and be of good cheer. | I pay my tenth before my money is spent. |
|---|---|---|---|
| When T.V. has a bad show, I turn it off and go! | Telling lies is so uncouth. Always tell the truth! | Bad words from me will not be heard. | If someone wants to pick a fight, turn and quickly get out of sight! |

My testimony of Jesus Christ helps me make right choices. Jesus "mint" for me to be happy, so I must follow Him.

What would Jesus do?

# Faithful Footsteps Flip Chart

I will follow in the footsteps of Jesus Christ.

I will endure to the end as I......

My prayer goals are:
_____
_____
_____
_____

👣 Pray to Heavenly Father

My tithing goals are:
_____
_____
_____
_____

👣 Pay my tithing

## Attend Church

My Church attendance goals are:
_____
_____
_____
_____
_____
_____

## Read the scriptures

My scripture reading goals are:
_____
_____
_____
_____
_____
_____

My "Choose the Right" goals are:

_____
_____
_____
_____
_____

Choose the Right

Be happy at home

Home is a better place to be

Steal or cheat

Lose the help of the Holy Ghost

Be kind to a new neighbor

Make a new friend

Pray

Receive Heavenly Father's help

Attend church

Learn the gospel

Tell a lie.

Others will not trust you

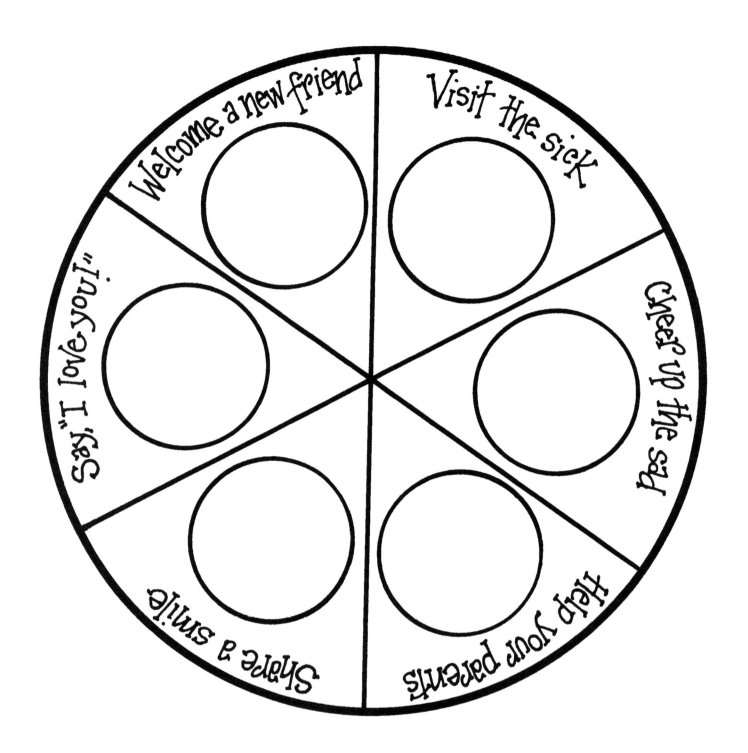

# Theme 7: I'll Follow Him in Faith—Galatians 3:26

**SONG:** Sing "Lord, I Would Follow Thee," *Children's Songbook,* page 220. This song is illustrated in *Primary Partners Singing Fun! I Belong to The Church of Jesus Christ of Latter-day Saints* book and CD-ROM.

Ask: "How can we follow Jesus in faith?"
Answer the question using the scriptures, Primary lessons, and sources below to teach.

---

**I Can Pray to Heavenly Father Anytime, Anywhere.**
**Heavenly Father Answers Our Prayers in Different Ways**
(Alma 34:19-27; *Primary 2,* lesson 10; *Primary 4,* lesson 37; *Primary 2,* lesson 18).
I can receive answers to my prayers (D&C 8:2; *Primary 2,* lesson 18; *Primary 4,* lesson 9).

---

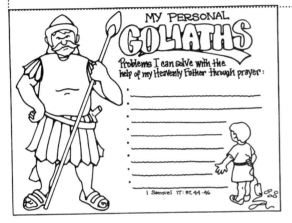

**Sharing Time Activity 1:**
Heavenly Father Helps Me as I Pray in Faith
(My Personal Goliaths Prayer Journal)

**TO MAKE:** *Copy, color, and cut out the *My Personal Goliaths Prayer Journal* (page 81).

**PREPARATION:** Review lesson 28 and enrichment activities 2, 3, and 4 (page 122) in the *Primary 6 Old Testament Manual.*

**ACTIVITY:** Talk about the courage David had to fight Goliath. Read: 1 Samuel 17:37 and 17:44-46. Have children take turns naming problems they can solve with the help of Heavenly Father through prayer (1 Samuel 17:37). Write these on the journal. **Examples:** School, family, friends, not having friends, feeling alone, other children making fun of them, not being able to talk to someone, not enough money.

**Sharing Time Activity 2:** I Will Seek Heavenly Father's Guidance (Puzzled About Prayer Crossword Puzzle)

**TO MAKE:** *Copy, color, and cut out the *Prayer Crossword Puzzle* (page 82).

**PREPARATION:** Review lesson 6 and enrichment activity 1 (page 28) in the *Primary 5 Doctrine and Covenants Manual.*

**ACTIVITY:** Have children take turns in teams or individually to complete this prayer crossword puzzle. *Objective:* To show children that answers to prayers come in many ways.
**Answer Key:** Across: 5—Heavenly Father, 7—ask, 8—morning, 9—listen, 10—thank, 15—still small voice, 17—help.
*Down:* 1—Holy Ghost, 2—prayer, 3—Jesus Christ, 4—yes, 6—guidance, 11—knees, 12—night, 13—blessings, 14—no, 18—peace.

*All images can be printed in full color or black and white using the CD-ROM: Primary Partners Teaching Tools—I Belong to The Church of Jesus Christ of Latter-day Saints.*

**I Can Learn More about Jesus and His Commandments as I Read the Scriptures**
(2 Nephi 32:3; *Primary 1*, lesson 41; *Primary 6*, lesson 37).

### Sharing Time Activity 3:
*Jesus Christ Performed Miracles (Three Miracles Picture Poster)*

**TO MAKE:** *Copy, color, and cut out the *Three Miracles Picture Poster* and pictures (pages 83-84).

**PREPARATION:** Review lesson 16 and the scripture accounts 1-3 (pages 54-55) in the *Primary 7 New Testament Manual*.

**ACTIVITY:** Strengthen children's faith in Jesus Christ by reading three miracles Jesus performed. Have children take turns finding the three pictures for each miracle and tape them in the right place, numbering the stickers 1, 2, and 3 to determine order of placement on the poster.

### Sharing Time Activity 4:
*I Will Be Blessed as I Read the Scriptures and Keep the Commandments (Sticker Challenge)*

**TO MAKE:** *Copy, color, and cut out the *Sticker Challenge* and pictures (pages 85-86).

**PREPARATION:** Review lesson 37 and the testimony (page 166) in the *Primary 6 Old Testament Manual*.

**ACTIVITY:** Ahead of time, give each class an assignment with the day of the week written at the top of their assignment, e.g., Sunday: 2 Chron. 34:51 and Mosiah 2:24 (reading the chart left to right). Ask teachers to have two different children present the two scriptures assigned. You will have a total of seven assignments with two scriptures each.

1. Tell children that they will be blessed as they read the scriptures each day, not just on Sunday or on Monday during family home evening. Say, "Let's learn how we are blessed from reading the scriptures."
2. "We have asked different classes to present their scriptures. Let's start with Sunday." (Call each class up by naming the day of the week.)

3. As children read the scripture, have them tape a "Read!" or "Blessings!" sticker to the right of the scripture it matches. Example: Place a "Read!" sticker next to the scriptures that tell you to read the scriptures. Place a "Blessings!" sticker next to the scripture that tells you blessings that come from reading the scriptures and obeying the commandments. The answers are shown in on the chart above.

*All images can be printed in full color or black and white using the CD-ROM:
*Primary Partners Teaching Tools—I Belong to The Church of Jesus Christ of Latter-day Saints.*

# Miracles of Jesus

Mark 2:1-12  Jesus heals a man with palsy.

Mark 5:21-24, 35-43  Jesus raises Jairus's daughter.

Mark 5:25-34  Jesus heals a woman.

# Scripture Blessings
## Sticker Challenge

|  | | | | |
|---|---|---|---|---|
| Sunday | 2 Chron. 34:31 | | Mosiah 2:24 | |
| Monday | Mosiah 2:41 | | 3 Nephi 10:14 | |
| Tuesday | D&C 18:8 | | Matthew 22:29 | |
| Wednesday | John 5:39 | | D&C 59:4 | |
| Thursday | 2 Tim. 3:15 | | D&C 104:2 | |
| Friday | D&C 124:90 | | D&C 68:1-4 | |
| Saturday | D&C 68:4 | | 2 Nephi 4:15 | |

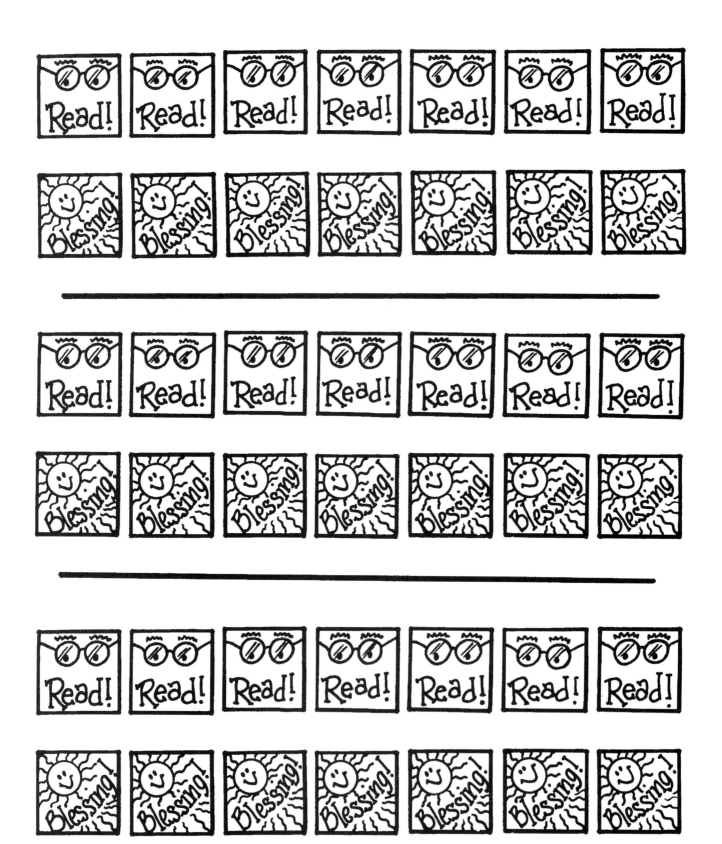

# Theme 8: I'll Honor His Name—Mosiah 5:8

**SONG:** Sing "Choose the Right Way," *Children's Songbook,* page 160. This song is illustrated in *Primary Partners Singing Fun! I Belong to The Church of Jesus Christ of Latter-day Saints* book and CD-ROM.

Ask: "How can we honor the name of Jesus Christ and Heavenly Father?"
Answer the question using the scriptures, Primary lessons, and sources below to teach.

> **I Take the Name of Jesus Christ upon Me When I Am Baptized**
> (D&C 18:22; 20:37; *Primary 4*, lessons 10, 12).

## Sharing Time Activity 1:
### I Will Be Valiant and Tell Others about Jesus (What Would Jesus Do? Choice Situation Sack)

For details and pattern see pages 61 and 71.

> **When I Take the Sacrament, I Renew My Baptismal Covenants: I Promise to Keep the Lord's Commandments and Always Remember Him** (D&C 20:77, 79; *Primary 3*, lesson 32, 33).

## Sharing Time Activity 2:
### I Will Think of Jesus (Testimony Building Blocks Puzzle)

**TO MAKE:** *Copy, color, and cut out the *Testimony Building Blocks Puzzle* wordstrips (page 90).

**PREPARATION:** Review lesson 29 and enrichment activity 3 (page 100) in the *Primary 7 New Testament Manual.*

**ACTIVITY:** Help children discover ways they can remember Jesus during the sacrament and in their daily life. Tape the wordstrips on the left and right of the board faceup. Post the "My Testimony Building Blocks" and "During the Sacrament" wordstrips at the top and the "In My Daily Life" wordstrip in center of the board or poster as shown above. Have children take turns drawing a wordstrip and placing it where it belongs to build the testimony puzzle.

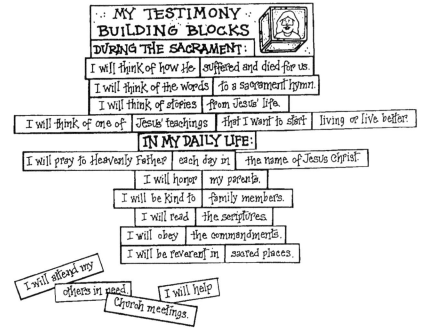

*All images can be printed in full color or black and white using the CD-ROM: Primary Partners Teaching Tools—I Belong to The Church of Jesus Christ of Latter-day Saints.*

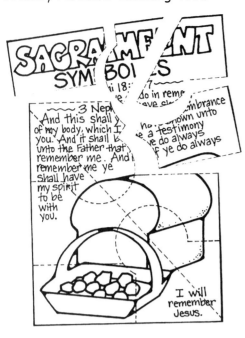

### Sharing Time Activity 3: I Will Remember Jesus (Sacrament Symbols Puzzles)

**TO MAKE:** *Copy, color, and cut out the *Sacrament Symbols Puzzles* (page 91).

**PREPARATION:** Review lesson 36 and enrichment activity 1 (page 130) and scripture discussion (pages 129-130) in the *Primary 4 Book of Mormon Manual.*

**ACTIVITY:** Have children help you put together the two puzzles and review the sacrament prayer. This will help children to always remember Jesus Christ and to strive to have His spirit to be with them. Place the puzzle pieces randomly to the left and right of the board. Have children take turns drawing a puzzle piece and placing it in the corresponding puzzle. *Team Activity:* Have two teams compete to see which team can put together both puzzles.

*About the Puzzles:* Side one of puzzle reminds children of the body (3 Nephi 18:7) and side two reminds children of the blood shed for them (3 Nephi 18:11). Help the children do side one of the puzzle, matching the scripture, then do side two. Tell them about Jesus bringing the sacrament to the Nephites.

### Sharing Time Activity 4: Heavenly Father Helps Me as I Obey (Commandment Concentration)

**TO MAKE:** *Copy, color, and cut out two sets of *Commandment Concentration* cards (page 92).

**PREPARATION:** Review lesson 3 and enrichment activity 5 (page 9) in the *Primary 4 Book of Mormon Manual.*

**ACTIVITY:** Play the *Commandment Concentration* game to remind children how they can obey the commandments to receive blessings from Heavenly Father.

*To Play:* Place the cards facedown on the board or table. Have a child come up from each class and turn over two cards to try to make a match. If a match is made, have that child tell how keeping this commandment can bring a blessing. If cards don't match, turn cards back over in the same position for the next player. Make sure that everyone sees both cards that are turned over before placing them back into position. Continue until last match is made or you run out of time.

---

*All images can be printed in full color or black and white using the CD-ROM: Primary Partners Teaching Tools—I Belong to The Church of Jesus Christ of Latter-day Saints.*

Primary Partners Teaching Tools — I Belong to The Church — Theme 8

**I Will Use the Names of Heavenly Father and Jesus Reverently** (Exodus 20:7; *Primary 3*, lesson 43).

**Sharing Time Activity 5:**
I Honor Heavenly Father, Jesus Christ, and the Holy Ghost (Worship Word Find)

**TO MAKE:** *Copy and color the *Whom Do I Worship? Word Find* (page 93).

**PREPARATION:** Review lesson 34 and enrichment activity 4 (page 152) in the *Primary 6 Old Testament Manual*.

**ACTIVITY:** Read the quote from the Prophet Ezra Taft Benson (*Ensign,* May, 1988, p. 5): "God our Father, Jesus, our Elder Brother and our Redeemer, and the Holy Ghost, the Testator, are perfect. They know us best and love us most and will not leave one thing undone for our eternal welfare." They want us to return to them.

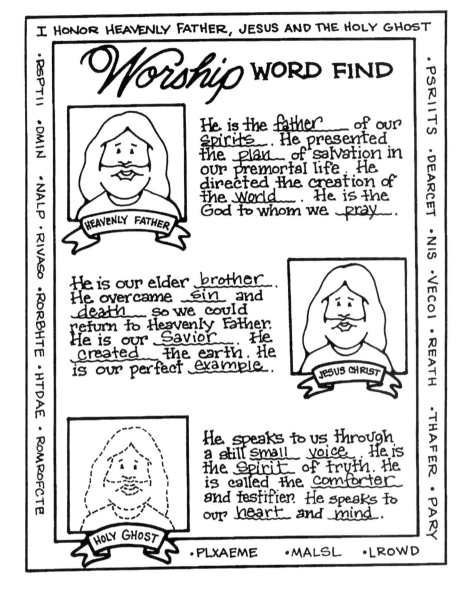

*To Do Word Find:*

1. Help children review the roles and titles of the three members of the Godhead with this backward word find.
2. Tell children that the clue words are along the sides, with the letters mixed up. Turn them around and write them in to learn whom they worship.

**Answers:** Heavenly Father: (Father, spirits, plan, world, pray) Jesus Christ: (brother, sin, death, Savior, created, example) Holy Ghost: (small voice, Spirit, comforter, heart and mind)

*All images can be printed in full color or black and white using the CD-ROM:
Primary Partners Teaching Tools—I Belong to The Church of Jesus Christ of Latter-day Saints.

# MY TESTIMONY BUILDING BLOCKS

## DURING THE SACRAMENT:

- I will think of how He suffered and died for us.
- I will think of the words to a sacrament hymn.
- I will think of stories from Jesus' life.
- I will think of one of Jesus' teachings that I want to start living or live better.

## IN MY DAILY LIFE:

- I will pray to Heavenly Father each day in the name of Jesus Christ.
- I will honor my parents.
- I will be kind to family members.
- I will read the scriptures.
- I will obey the commandments.
- I will be reverent in sacred places.
- I will help others in need.
- I will attend my Church meetings.

I HONOR HEAVENLY FATHER, JESUS AND THE HOLY GHOST

# Worship WORD FIND

HEAVENLY FATHER

He is the _____ of our _____. He presented the _____ of salvation in our premortal life. He directed the creation of the _____. He is the God to whom we _____.

He is our elder _____. He overcame _____ and _____ so we could return to Heavenly Father. He is our _____. He _____ the earth. He is our perfect _____.

JESUS CHRIST

HOLY GHOST

He speaks to us through a still _____ _____. He is the _____ of truth. He is called the _____ and testifier. He speaks to our _____ and _____.

Side word scramble list (left): •RSPT1I •DMIN •NALP •RIVASO •RORBHTE •HTDAE •RoMRoFCTE

Side word scramble list (right): •PSRIITS •DEARCET •NIS •VECoI •REATH •THAFER •PARY

Bottom: •PLXAEME •MALSL •LROWD

# Theme 9: I'll Do What is Right—Deuteronomy 6:18

**SONG:** Sing "Kindness Begins with Me," *Children's Songbook*, page 145.
Ask: "What choices do we make when we do what is right?"
Answer the questions using the scriptures, Primary lessons, and sources below to teach.

**I Can Know When the Holy Ghost Is Helping Me Choose the Right**
(Moroni 10:5; *Primary 3*, lesson 26; *Primary 6*, lesson 27).

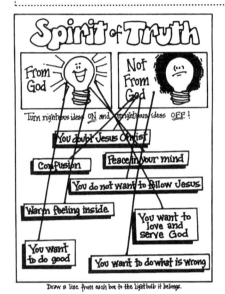

**Sharing Time Activity 1:** Jesus Speaks to Me Through the Holy Ghost (Spirit of Truth Cross Match)

**TO MAKE:** *Copy, color, and cut out the *Find the Spirit of Truth Cross Match* (page 97).
**PREPARATION:** Review lesson 27 and enrichment activity 2 (page 119) in the *Primary 6 Old Testament Manual*.
**ACTIVITY:** Help children know the difference between righteous ideas (ideas from God) and unrighteous ideas (ideas not from God). Explain that ideas are like a light going on inside our mind. The light that comes from God is a bright light that brings a warm, happy feeling. The dim light that is not from God brings a cold, sad feeling.
**To Do Cross Match:** Draw a line from each box to the lightbulb where it belongs. **Answers And Additional Scripture Reading:**
IDEAS FROM GOD: D&C 9:8 (warm feeling inside), Moroni 7:13 (you want to do good), Moroni 7:13 (you want to love and serve God), D&C 6:23 and John 14:27 (peace in your mind)
IDEAS NOT FROM GOD: D&C 9:9 (confusion), Moroni 7:17 (you want to do wrong, you do not want to follow Jesus, you doubt Jesus Christ)

**Choose One or Two of the Principles from *My Gospel Standards* to Present Each Week.**

**Sharing Time Activity 2:**
I Will Live Worthy to Receive Priesthood Blessings (My Gospel Standards Sentence Search)

**TO MAKE:** *Copy and color the *My Gospel Standards Sentence Search* (page 98).
**PREPARATION:** Review lesson 47 and enrichment activities 1 and 4 (pages 214-216) in the *Primary 6 Old Testament Manual*.
**ACTIVITY:** Help children learn the gospel standards they are asked to follow by completing the following sentence search.
**To Do Sentence Search:** To find the complete the Gospel Standard sentence; match the first column lines with the second column lines

*All images can be printed in full color or black and white using the CD-ROM:
Primary Partners Teaching Tools—I Belong to The Church of Jesus Christ of Latter-day Saints.

Primary Partners Teaching Tools — I Belong to The Church — Theme 9

by writing the number in the center circle. Example: The partial statement "*I will remember my baptismal covenants and*" matches with 7 "*listen to the Holy Ghost.*" Place the number "7" in the center circle.

**Answers** (Numbers to place in circles): 7, 11, 1, 9, 2 or 8, 2 or 8, 3, 5, 4, 13, 6, 10, 12

Let children know that as they follow these gospel standards, they will be worthy to receive priesthood blessings. Review lesson 33 (page 147) in *Primary* 6 manual. Priesthood Blessings We Can Receive by Living the Gospel Standards: • Blessing Babies • Baptism • Laying on of Hands for the Gift of the Holy Ghost • Sacrament • Administration to the Sick • Father's Blessings • Ordination to the Priesthood • Temple Ordinances • Being Set Apart for Missions or Callings

## Sharing Time Activity 3: I Will Make and Keep Good Promises (Honesty Pays Blessings Bucks Board Game)

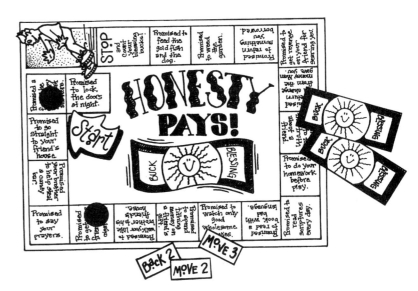

**TO MAKE:** *Copy, color, and cut out the *Honesty Pays Blessing Bucks Board Game* (pages 99-100).

**PREPARATION:** Review lesson 14 and the enrichment activity 2 (page 58) in the *Primary 6 Old Testament Manual.*

**ACTIVITY:** Help children learn the difference between good promises and bad promises. Even though children may be honest about keeping their promises, some promises are good and some are bad. Blessings come from keeping good promises. Play, following the rules (found on the pattern). Tell children that the word "bucks" means money (in paper bills), which is a temporal reward, but Blessing Bucks are spiritual rewards that come from making and keeping good promises. Honesty pays because they feel good about the promises they make and others trust them.

## Sharing Time Activity 4: I Can Be a True Friend to Jesus and Others (Fishing for a Friend Spin-and-Tell)

**TO MAKE:** *Copy, color, and cut out the *Fishing for a Friend Spin-and-Tell* and "true blue" friend notes (pages 101-102).

**REPARATION:** Review lesson 29, the attention activity (p. 125), and enrichment activities 2 and 4 (p. 128) in the *Primary 6 Old Test. Manual.*

**ACTIVITY:** Help children learn the qualities of a "true blue" friend. Have children take turns spinning the fish. Do one of the three things: Tell something about yourself so others can know more about you. Tell something you know and like about someone in the circle. Fish for a "true blue" friend note and read what a true friend does. ("True blue" friend notes should be placed facedown a pile in the center to draw from.)

*All images can be printed in full color or black and white using the CD-ROM:
*Primary Partners Teaching Tools—I Belong to The Church of Jesus Christ of Latter-day Saints.*

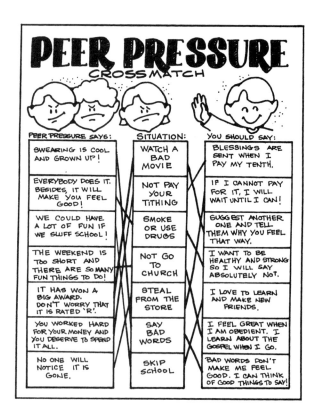

## Sharing Time Activity 5:
### I Will Be a Positive Influence on My Friends (Peer Pressure Cross Match Puzzle)

**TO MAKE:** *Copy, color, and cut out the *Peer Pressure Cross Match Puzzle* (page 103).

**PREPARATION:** Review lesson 32 and enrichment activity 1 (page 142) in the *Primary 6 Old Testament Manual*.

**ACTIVITY:** Read the quote from Robert D. Hales (*Ensign*, May 1990, page 40): "A true friend makes it easier for us to live the gospel by being around him." Help children learn how to respond to peer pressure situations, to be a positive influence on their friends.

***To Do Cross Match:***

1. Draw an arrow from the pressure situation (listed in the center column) to the left (negative peer pressure).
2. Then draw an arrow from the pressure situation to the right (positive influence). Talk about the consequences for each decision.

## Sharing Time Activity 6: I Will Keep this Law of Health (Word of Wisdom Choices Match Puzzle)

**TO MAKE:** *Copy, color, and cut out the *Word of Wisdom Choices Match Puzzle* (page 104) on colored paper for each child; pencils, tape, and markers.

**PREPARATION:** Review lesson 40 and enrichment activity 1 (page 177) in the *Primary 6 Old Testament Manual*.

**ACTIVITY:** Help children think of the Word of Wisdom choices. Learn which choices make us happy and healthy and which choices make us sad and unhealthy.

***To Do Puzzle Match:*** Read instructions on puzzle to match up pictures and draw smile and frown faces. Draw a straight face on D&C 89:12 (as it tells us that meat should be eaten *"sparingly"*).

***Teaching Tool:*** Place pictures next to scriptures so the scriptures show, or tape them over the scriptures at the top to create a flap. Encourage children to share this with their family.

*All images can be printed in full color or black and white using the CD-ROM: Primary Partners Teaching Tools—I Belong to The Church of Jesus Christ of Latter-day Saints.

# Spirit of Truth

Turn righteous ideas ON and unrighteous ideas OFF!

- You doubt Jesus Christ
- Confusion
- Peace in your mind
- You do not want to follow Jesus
- Warm feeling inside
- You want to love and serve God
- You want to do good
- You want to do what is wrong

Draw a line from each box to the lightbulb it belongs to.

# MY GOSPEL STANDARDS

Find the complete Gospel Standards sentence. Match the first column lines with the second and write your answer in the center circle.

|  |  |
|---|---|
| I will remember my baptismal covenants and... | 1. ...treat others kindly. |
| I will be honest with... | 2. ...pleasing to Heavenly Father |
| I will seek good friends and... | 3. ...reverently. I will not swear or use crude words. |
| I will dress modestly to show respect for... | 4. ...harmful. |
| I will only read and watch things that are... | 5. ...body sacred and pure. |
| I will only listen to music that is... | 6. ...repent when I make a mistake. |
| I will use the name of Heavenly Father and Jesus Christ... | 7. ...listen to the Holy Ghost. |
| I will keep my mind and... | 8. ...pleasing to Heavenly Father. |
| I will not partake of things that are... | 9. ...Heavenly Father and myself. |
| I will do those things on the Sabbath that will... | 10. ...the temple and serve a mission. |
| I will choose the right. I know I can... | 11. ...Heavenly Father, others and myself. |
| I will live now to be worthy to go to... | 12. ...plan for me. |
| I will follow Heavenly Father's... | 13. ...help me feel close to Heavenly Father. |

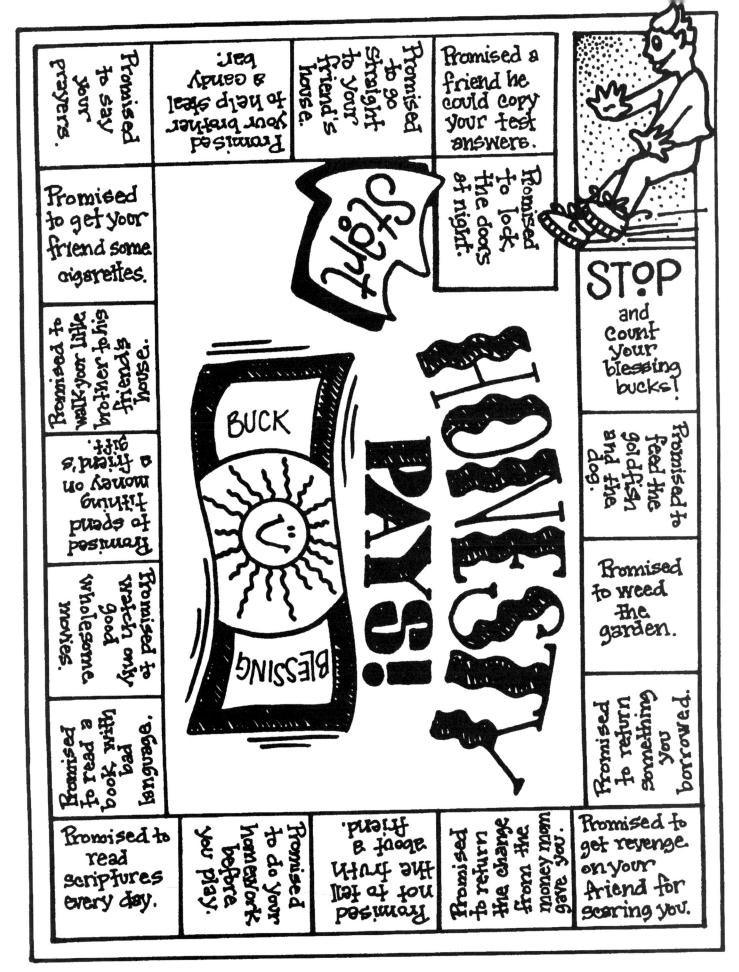

**GAME RULES:** (1) Divide children into two teams, using buttons or coins for markers at the START position. (2) Take turns drawing a move marker and moving to that position on the board. (3) Read the promise and decide if it is a good promise or a bad promise. If it is a bad promise, tell what the consequence is for making that bad promise. If it is a good promise, tell what the consequence is for following through on a good promise, and collect a Blessing Buck. (4) When someone reaches "STOP," add up the Blessing Bucks to determine winner!

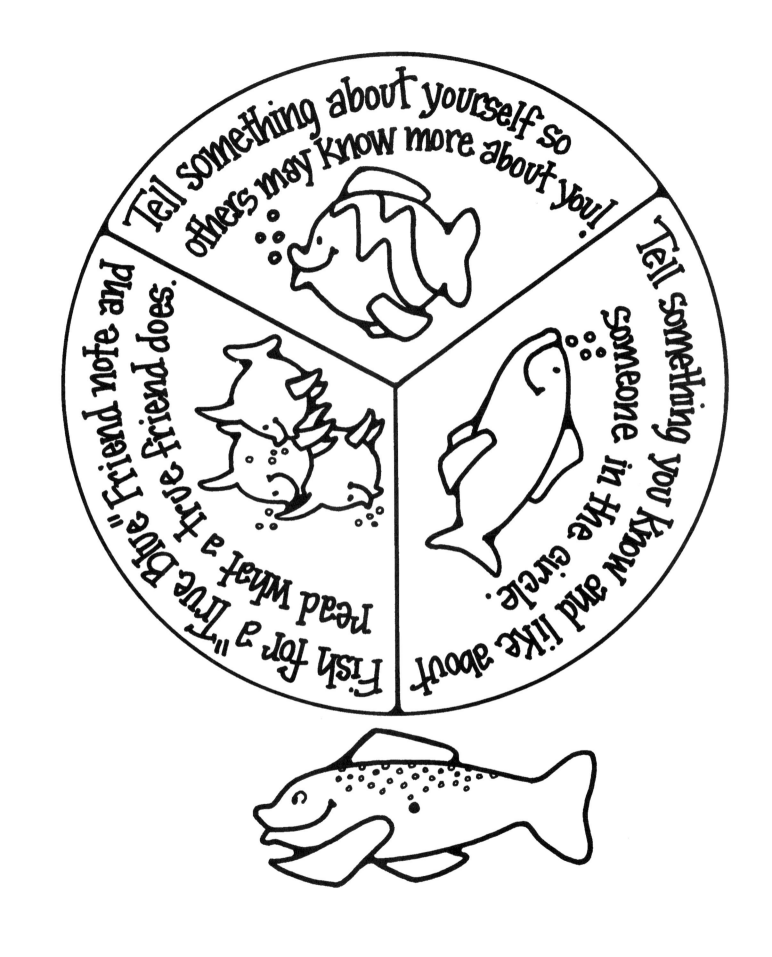

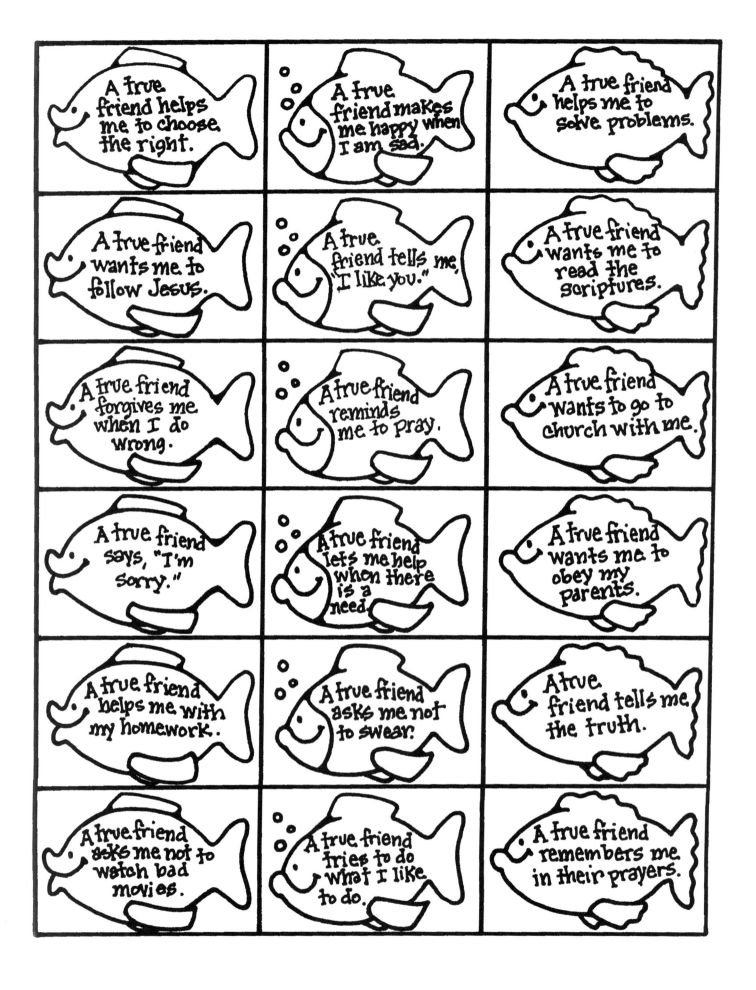

# PEER PRESSURE
## CROSS MATCH

| PEER PRESSURE SAYS: | SITUATION: | YOU SHOULD SAY: |
|---|---|---|
| SWEARING IS COOL AND GROWN UP! | WATCH A BAD MOVIE | BLESSINGS ARE SENT WHEN I PAY MY TENTH. |
| EVERYBODY DOES IT. BESIDES, IT WILL MAKE YOU FEEL GOOD! | NOT PAY YOUR TITHING | IF I CANNOT PAY FOR IT, I WILL WAIT UNTIL I CAN! |
| WE COULD HAVE A LOT OF FUN IF WE SLUFF SCHOOL! | SMOKE OR USE DRUGS | SUGGEST ANOTHER ONE AND TELL THEM WHY YOU FEEL THAT WAY. |
| THE WEEKEND IS TOO SHORT AND THERE ARE SO MANY FUN THINGS TO DO! | NOT GO TO CHURCH | I WANT TO BE HEALTHY AND STRONG SO I WILL SAY ABSOLUTELY NOT! |
| IT HAS WON A BIG AWARD. DON'T WORRY THAT IT IS RATED 'R'. | STEAL FROM THE STORE | I LOVE TO LEARN AND MAKE NEW FRIENDS. |
| YOU WORKED HARD FOR YOUR MONEY AND YOU DESERVE TO SPEND IT ALL. | SAY BAD WORDS | I FEEL GREAT WHEN I AM OBEDIENT. I LEARN ABOUT THE GOSPEL WHEN I GO. |
| NO ONE WILL NOTICE IT IS GONE. | SKIP SCHOOL | BAD WORDS DON'T MAKE ME FEEL GOOD. I CAN THINK OF GOOD THINGS TO SAY! |

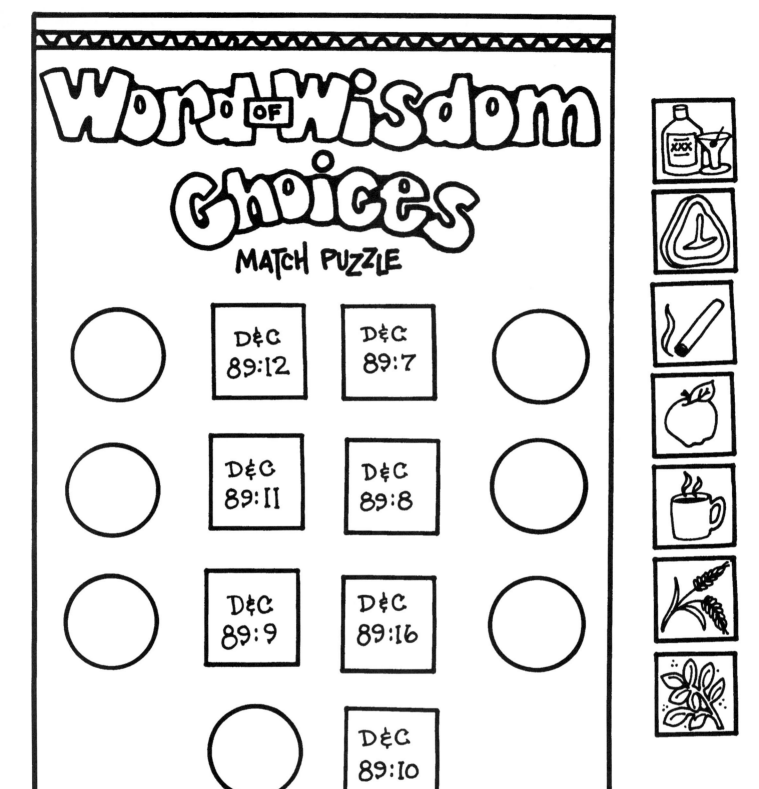

# Theme 10: I'll Follow His Light—John 14:6

**SONGS:** Sing "Tell Me the Stories of Jesus," page 57, "Shine On," page 144, and "Keep the Commandments," page 146, from the *Children's Songbook*.

Ask: "How can we follow Jesus who is our light?"
Answer the question using the scriptures, Primary lessons, and sources below to teach.

---

**Jesus Lights the Way as My Example** (3 Nephi 18:16).

---

## Sharing Time Activity 1: I Will Follow Jesus (Footstep Flash Cards)

**TO MAKE:** *Copy, color, and cut out two sets of *Footstep Flash Cards* (pages 108-109).

**PREPARATION:** Review lesson 23 and enrichment activity 1 (page 77) in the *Primary 7 New Testament Manual*.

**ACTIVITY:** (1) Review *Footstep Flash Cards* 1-12 with children. Tell children that Jesus wants us to follow in His footsteps because He knows the way to eternal happiness.
(2) Tape two sets of footstep flash cards 1-12 facedown on the board. (3) Play a match game by dividing children into two teams, taking turns turning cards over to make a match. The team with the most matches wins.

---

**Jesus Lights the Ways with His Teachings** (D&C 84:45-46; *Primary 7*, lessons 10, 12).

---

## Sharing Time Activity 2: Others Testify That Jesus Is God's Son (Testimonies of Jesus Scripture Picture Match Game)

**TO MAKE:** *Copy, color, and cut out the *Testimonies of Jesus Scripture Picture Match* cards (pages 110-111).

**PREPARATION:** Review lesson 28 and enrichment activities 2 and 3 (page 97) in the *Primary 7 New Testament Manual*.

**ACTIVITIES:** Help children look up the scriptures and learn events where someone witnessed that Jesus Christ is the Son of God. Review the instructions (on the pattern page) to make and play the game. Place match cards in a zip-close plastic bag, along with the "Testimonies of Jesus Christ" label and game rules. Enlarge cards if using for sharing time.

*All images can be printed in full color or black and white using the CD-ROM:
*Primary Partners Teaching Tools—I Belong to The Church of Jesus Christ of Latter-day Saints.*

## Sharing Time Activity 3: Jesus Taught Us How to Return to Heaven ("Bee"-atitude Cross Match)

**TO MAKE:** *Copy and color the "Bee"-atitude Cross Match (page 112).

**PREPARATION:** Review lesson 10 and enrichment activity 7 (page 35) in the *Primary 7 New Testament Manual*.

**ACTIVITY:** Tell children that Jesus taught the Beatitudes in His Sermon on the Mount, showing us how we can return to heaven. Help children learn the beatitudes (Matthew 5:3-12) and then match the beatitude with the bee. Compare the New Testament references with the Book of Mormon and write in the translation. See *References* below. Example: *"Blessed are the poor in spirit"* (*"who come unto me"* was left out in the Bible but was given in 3 Nephi 12:3). Remind children of the 8th Article of Faith: *"We believe the Bible to be the word of God as far as it is translated correctly; we also believe the Book of Mormon to be the word of God."* Explain that Jesus gave the Beatitudes while He was living on the earth in the New Testament times. After His death and resurrection, He visited the Nephites on the American continent and gave them the Beatitudes (3 Nephi).

*References:* ❤ Matthew 5:3 (missing a part found in 3 Nephi 12:3, *"who come unto me"*) ❤ Matthew 5:6 (missing a part found in 3 Nephi 12:6, *"filled with the Holy Ghost"*) ❤ See the cross references below 3 Nephi 2:10 (Matthew 5:10 and D&C 122:5-9 telling that Joseph Smith was persecuted for righteousness' sake) ❤ Matthew 5:48 and 3 Nephi 12:48 (become *"perfect"* is to become like Heavenly Father and Jesus).

## Sharing Time Activity 4: The Gospel of Jesus Christ Is My Sure Foundation (Rock and Body Puzzle)

**TO MAKE:** *Copy, color, and cut out the *puzzle* (page 113).

**PREPARATION:** Review lesson 12 and enrichment activity 3 (page 43) in the *Primary 7 New Testament Manual*.

**ACTIVITY:** Have children help you put together the puzzle to show ways they can obey the commandments, showing that the gospel of Jesus Christ is our rock. Read, *"Build upon my rock, which is my gospel"* (D&C 11:24), and tell children that Jesus is the rock. He is our Redeemer, the Son of God. We must build a firm foundation by living the gospel of Jesus Christ, or we will not have the power to overcome the mighty winds and storms of the devil, who would *"drag you down into the gulf of misery and endless woe."* (Read Helaman 5:12.)

*All images can be printed in full color or black and white using the CD-ROM: Primary Partners Teaching Tools—I Belong to The Church of Jesus Christ of Latter-day Saints.

**I Will Follow His Light and Be an Example** (3 Nephi 18:24; *Primary 1*, lesson 36; *Primary 2*, lesson 29).

## Sharing Time Activity 5: I Can Follow Jesus and Obey (Heavenly Treasure Hunt)

**TO MAKE:** *Copy, color, and cut out the *Heavenly Treasure Hunt* (page 114). Color and cut out treasure label and cards.

**PREPARATION:** Review lesson 30 and the enrichment activity 4 (page 159) in the *Primary 2-CTR A Manual*.

**ACTIVITY:** Have a treasure hunt to find a treasure bag filled with obedience reminder cards to inspire children to be obedient and follow Jesus. This way they can receive the greatest treasure, to live with Heavenly Father again.

*Treasure Hunt:* Send two children out of the room and ask another child to hide (tape) the treasure sack under a chair or somewhere in the room. Have the children come back in and search for the treasure. If they need coaxing, the other children can say they are getting hot, if they are getting close, or cold and colder if they are getting further away. After they have found the special treasure, say, "If we obey and follow the Savior, we live with Heavenly Father. This is our greatest treasure."

**As I Follow His Light, I Am Protected**
(Psalm 27:1; *Primary 4*, lessons 25, 26).

## Sharing Time Activity 6: The Armor of God Will Protect Me from Evil (Fight for Right! Word Choice)

**TO MAKE:** *Copy and color the *Fight for Right! Word Choice* (page 115).

**PREPARATION:** Review lesson 25 and enrichment activity 3 (page 87) in the *Primary 4 Book of Mormon Manual*.

**ACTIVITY:** Show children how they can fight for right! and follow Captain Moroni's example to put on the whole armor of God. Help them search for and black out wrong choices to see ways they can fight for right!

*All images can be printed in full color or black and white using the CD-ROM: *Primary Partners Teaching Tools—I Belong to The Church of Jesus Christ of Latter-day Saints*.

| Footstep Flash Card #1 | Footstep Flash Card #2 | Footstep Flash Card #3 |
|---|---|---|
| Jesus Was Born of Mary | Jesus Was Baptized by Immersion | Jesus Chose 12 Apostles |
|  |  |  |
| Footstep Flash Card #4 | Footstep Flash Card #5 | Footstep Flash Card #6 |
| Jesus Gave Sermon on the Mount | Jesus Taught Us to Pray | Jesus Healed the Sick |
|  |  |  |

| Footstep Flash Card #7 | Footstep Flash Card #8 | Footstep Flash Card #9 |
|---|---|---|
| Jesus Fed the 5,000 | Jesus is Our Shepherd | Jesus Told Parables |
| 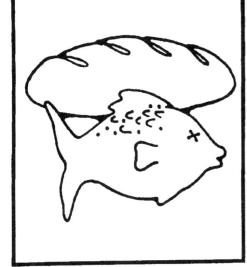 |  | 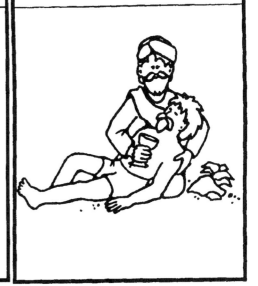 |
| Footstep Flash Card #10 | Footstep Flash Card #11 | Footstep Flash Card #12 |
| Jesus Blessed the Children | Jesus Suffered for Our Sins | Jesus Died and Was Resurrected |
|  |  |  |

Testimonies of Jesus Christ

Picture - Scripture Match Game

**TO MAKE MATCH GAME:**
1. Color and cut out cards.
2. Look up scriptures and fill in the missing words, talking about the event. Look at the matching picture as you talk about the event.

**TO PLAY MATCH GAME:**
1. Mix and lay cards face down on the floor.
2. Divide into two teams sitting across from each other in a circle.
3. Take turns turning cards over to make a match. The team with the most matches wins! If every player has not had a turn, play the game again.

---

EVENT THAT TESTIFIES OF JESUS CHRIST:

Jesus Raised Lazarus from the

---

John 11:25

"Jesus said unto her, I am the __ __ __ __ __ __ __ __ __ __ __ __, and the __ __ __ __ __: he that __ __ __ __ __ __ __ __ __ in me, though he were __ __ __ __ __, yet shall he __ __ __ __."

(Jesus was speaking to Martha, the sister of Lazarus)

---

EVENT THAT TESTIFIES OF JESUS CHRIST:

Jesus Was Born

---

Luke 2:11

"An angel said, Unto you is __ __ __ __ this day in the city of __ __ __ __ __ __ a __ __ __ __ __ __ __, which is Christ the __ __ __ __."

---

EVENT THAT TESTIFIES OF JESUS CHRIST:

Jesus Was Baptized

---

Mark 1:11

"There was a __ __ __ __ __ from heaven saying, "Thou art my __ __ __ __ __ __ __ Son"; the Spirit of God descended like a dove.

| | |
|---|---|
| EVENT THAT TESTIFIES OF JESUS CHRIST:<br><br>Jesus Walked on the Water  | Matthew 14:25-27, 32-33<br><br>"In the fourth watch of the night Jesus went unto them, __ __ __ __ __ __ __ on the __ __ __." Jesus' disciples on the ship said, "Of a truth thou art the __ __ __ of __ __ __." |
| EVENT THAT TESTIFIES OF JESUS CHRIST:<br><br>Jesus Healed a Man Born Blind  | John 9:32, 35-38<br><br>"And [the man] said, __ __ __ __, I __ __ __ __ __ __ __ [you are the Son of God]. And he worshipped him." |
| EVENT THAT TESTIFIES OF JESUS CHRIST:<br><br>Peter Testified of Christ  | Matthew 16:13-16<br><br>When Jesus asked his disciples who they thought he was, Peter said,<br>"Thou art the __ __ __ __ __ __, the Son of the __ __ __ __ __ God." |
| EVENT THAT TESTIFIES OF JESUS CHRIST:<br><br>Joseph Smith Receives His First Vision  | Joseph Smith—History 1:17<br><br>Heavenly Father said, "This is My __ __ __ __ __ __ __ __ Son. __ __ __ __ Him!" |

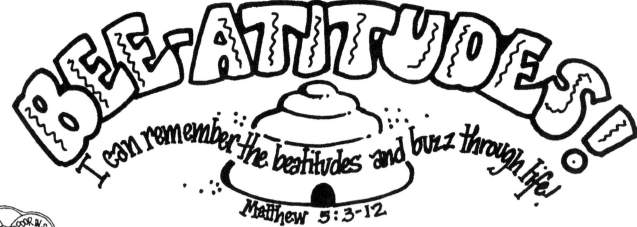

# BEE-ATITUDES!
*I can remember the beatitudes and buzz through life!*
Matthew 5:3-12

 Blessed are the poor in spirit.... ○ for they shall inherit the earth.

 Blessed are they which do hunger and thirst after righteousness... ○ for they shall obtain mercy.

 Blessed are the pure in heart.... ○ for theirs is the Kingdom of heaven.

 Blessed are the meek.... ○ for they shall be comforted.

 Blessed are the merciful... ○ for they shall be filled.

 Blessed are they that mourn.... ○ for they shall be called the children of God.

 Blessed are the peacemakers... ○ for they shall see God.

# Theme 11: Teachings of the Prophet—Amos 3:7

**SONGS:** Sing "Remember the Sabbath," page 155, "We'll Bring the World His Truth," page 172, and "Follow the Prophet," page 110 in the *Children's Songbook*.

Ask: "What are the blessings we receive from obeying the prophet's counsel given at general conference?" Answer the question using the scriptures, Primary lessons, and sources below to teach.

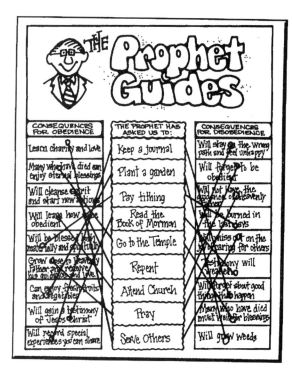

## Sharing Time Activity 1:
### I Will Listen to the Prophet (The Prophet Guides Choices and Consequences Cross Match)

**TO MAKE:** *Copy and color *The Prophet Guides Choices and Consequences Cross Match* (page 118).

**PREPARATION:** Review lesson 31 and enrichment activity 2 (page 178) in the *Primary 5 Doctrine and Covenants/Church History Manual*.

**ACTIVITY:** Help children realize the good and bad consequences that come from our choices by doing *The Prophet Guides Choices and Consequences Cross Match*.

1. Draw an arrow from the action the prophet has asked us to do to the left and right side. The left side shows good consequences that come from obeying. The right side shows bad consequences that come from not obeying the prophet.
2. Explain that there is always a good or bad consequence for our decisions to listen to or reject the words of the living prophet.
3. Review each choice and its consequences, having children share experiences and stories that relate.
4. Share scriptures that relate to the choices made and their consequences.

## Sharing Time Activity 2: I Will Trust in the Lord and Obey (Follow Righteous Leaders Trust-and-Tell Game)

**TO MAKE:** (1) Create a sign to post on the board by enlarging the "Follow Righteous Leaders" label (page 119). (2) Create a wordstrip bag by copying actual size the "Follow Righteous Leaders" label and wordstrips. Color the label and cut out the wordstrips, placing label and wordstrips in the bag. Glue the rules on the back of the label. (3) Create a bean bag by filling a zip-close sandwich bag with beans, zipping closed, and placing a second bag over the top for durability.

**PREPARATION:** Review lesson 24 and enrichment activities 1 and 3 (page 108) in the *Primary 6 Old Testament Manual*.

**ACTIVITY:** Help children learn to trust and follow righteous leaders. Follow the rules on the pattern page to play the game.

*All images can be printed in full color or black and white using the CD-ROM: Primary Partners Teaching Tools—I Belong to The Church of Jesus Christ of Latter-day Saints.

Primary Partners Teaching Tools — I Belong to The Church — Theme 11

### Sharing Time Activity 3: I Will Stay on the Right Road to Happiness (Valiantville "Convert"-able Obstacle Course)

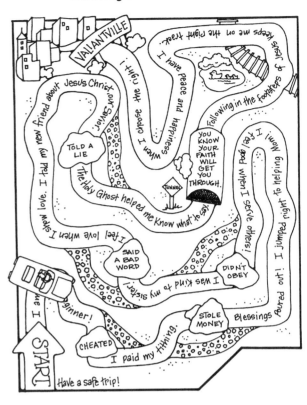

**TO MAKE:** *Copy and color the *Valiantville "Convert"-able Obstacle Course* and car (page 120) and cut out the car. *Note:* *Color obstacle course in a pale shade, e.g., yellow or peach so not to cover the words.

**PREPARATION:** Review lesson 42 and enrichment activity 5 (page 149) in the *Primary 7 New Testament Manual*.

**ACTIVITY:** Talk to children about taking the right and wrong turns in life and where they might lead.
*To Play Game:* Take turns tossing a coin (heads = one sentence forward, tails = one sentence backward. The first team to get to Valiantville wins!
*Travel Tips:* Travel through this obstacle course as a class or individually with your own private car. As you start, you are on testimony trail. Try to move to Valiantville to find happiness. Valiantville is Zion, the city of eternal happiness. To take your journey, move your "convert"-able car as you go about getting converted. When an obstacle (big rock) comes, say "no" to temptation. To get back on the road, back out onto repentance road (the bumpy path). Remember that this road is not smooth. It can be rough to repent, but it is worth it to turn your life around. You will feel better when you are back on testimony trail.

### Sharing Time Activity 4: The Gospel of Jesus Christ Is True (Valiant Testimony Board Game)

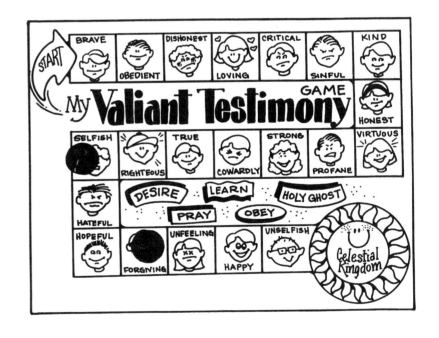

**TO MAKE:** *Copy, color, and cut out the *Valiant Testimony Board Game* (pages 121-123).

**PREPARATION:** Review lesson 41 and enrichment activity 4 (page 183) in the *Primary 6 Old Testament Manual*.

**ACTIVITY:** (1) Help children learn ways they can strengthen their testimonies of Jesus Christ and His gospel. See game rules and answers (on the pattern).
(2) Post the game board on the board to present. (3) Divide children into two teams using the circle paper markers to mark their place. Tape double-stick tape or fun tack on the back of markers to move on game pieces and suspend them on the board.

*All images can be printed in full color or black and white using the CD-ROM:
*Primary Partners Teaching Tools—I Belong to The Church of Jesus Christ of Latter-day Saints.*

# The Prophet Guides

Draw an arrow from the action (center) to the consequences for obedience (left) and the consequences for disobedience (right). Remember to follow the Prophet!

| CONSEQUENCES FOR OBEDIENCE | THE PROPHET HAS ASKED US TO: | CONSEQUENCES FOR DISOBEDIENCE |
|---|---|---|
| Learn charity and love | Keep a journal | Will stay on the wrong path and feel unhappy |
| Many who have died can enjoy eternal blessings | Plant a garden | Will forget to be obedient |
| Will cleanse spirit and start new actions | Pay tithing | Will not have the guidance of Heavenly Father |
| Will learn how to be obedient | Read the Book of Mormon | Will be burned in the last days |
| Will be blessed both materially and spiritually | Go to the Temple | Will miss out on the joy of caring for others |
| Grow close to Heavenly Father and receive His guidance and love. | Repent | Testimony will weaken |
| Can enjoy fresh fruits and vegetables | Attend Church | Will forget about good things that happen |
| Will gain a testimony of Jesus Christ | Pray | Many who have died must wait for blessings |
| Will record special experiences you can share | Serve Others | Will grow weeds |

**GAME RULES**
1. Players stand in a circle.
2. Toss the bag to a person standing in the circle.
3. That person draws a CTR Challenge wordstrip out of the bag and reads it aloud. This is a temptation we might face. *Option:* Instead of drawing a wordstrip, name a tempting situation on your own.
4. That person tells others what a trusted righteous leader would ask you to do. Example: CTR Challenge: "Asked to smoke a cigarette." A righteous leader says: "Obey the Word of Wisdom."

---

CTR CHALLENGE: **ASKED TO SMOKE A CIGARETTE.** RIGHTEOUS LEADER SAYS:
_____

CTR CHALLENGE: **ASKED TO TAKE DRUGS.** RIGHTEOUS LEADER SAYS:
_____

CTR CHALLENGE: **ASKED TO DRINK BEER.** RIGHTEOUS LEADER SAYS:
_____

CTR CHALLENGE: **TEMPTED NOT TO READ SCRIPTURES.** RIGHTEOUS LEADER SAYS:
_____

CTR CHALLENGE: **ASKED TO SHOP ON SUNDAY.** RIGHTEOUS LEADER SAYS:
_____

CTR CHALLENGE: **ASKED TO STEAL SOMETHING.** RIGHTEOUS LEADER SAYS:
_____

CTR CHALLENGE: **TEMPTED TO CHEAT ON A TEST.** RIGHTEOUS LEADER SAYS:
_____

CTR CHALLENGE: **TEMPTED NOT TO PRAY.** RIGHTEOUS LEADER SAYS:
_____

CTR CHALLENGE: **TEMPTED TO SKIP CHURCH.** RIGHTEOUS LEADER SAYS:
_____

CTR CHALLENGE: **TEMPTED TO SPEND TITHING MONEY.** RIGHTEOUS LEADER SAYS:
_____

CTR CHALLENGE: **TEMPTED TO TELL A LIE.** RIGHTEOUS LEADER SAYS:
_____

CTR CHALLENGE: **TEMPTED TO SWEAR.** RIGHTEOUS LEADER SAYS:
_____

CTR CHALLENGE: **TEMPTED TO TALK DURING SACRAMENT MEETING.** RIGHTEOUS LEADER SAYS:
_____

CTR CHALLENGE: **TEMPTED TO NOT HELP AT HOME.** RIGHTEOUS LEADER SAYS:
_____

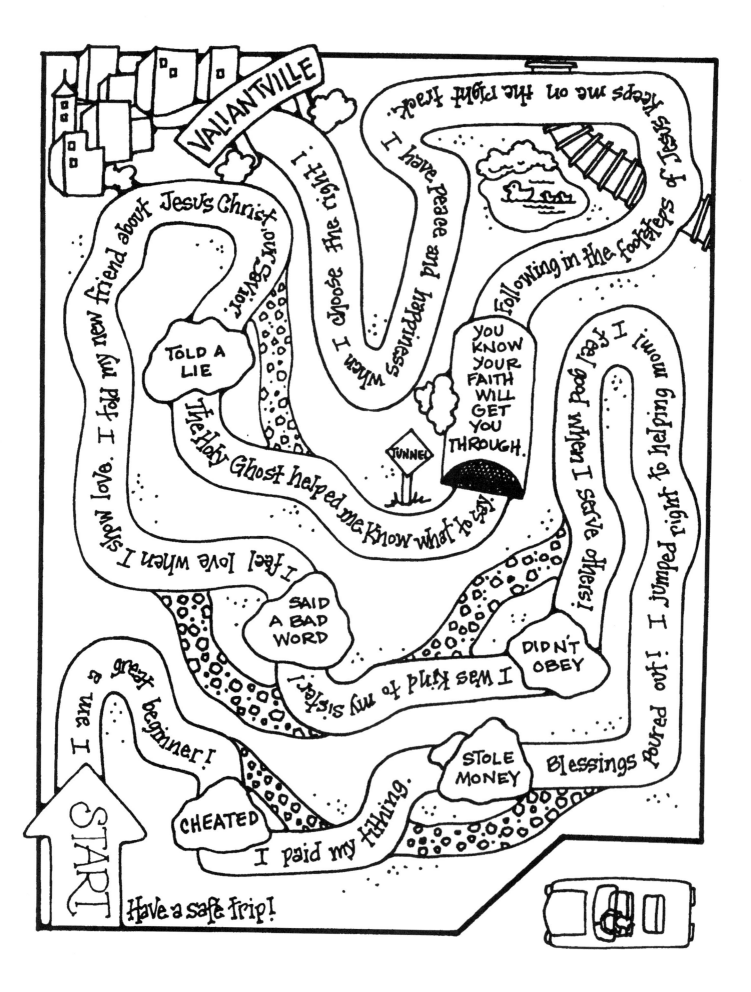

## How to Play "My Valiant Testimony" Game:

1. Divide into two teams.
2. Mix up testimony cards 1-42 and place facedown.
3. Use a coin or button marker for each team and place on START.
4. Take turns drawing number (1, 2, or 3) wordstrips out of a container and move that number of spaces on the board.
5. If you land on an non-valiant action word (with frowny face), move back one space.
6. If you land on a valiant action word (with smile face), draw a testimony card.
7. Read the testimony card and guess the missing keyword (found on the game board): DESIRE, PRAY, LEARN, OBEY, or HOLY GHOST.
8. Place card in a pile until all wordstrips are read, then place wordstrips back in container to play again.
9. Score 10 points for guessing the keyword right. See answers listed below.
10. The first team to reach Celestial Kingdom wins, or the first team to earn 100 points.

**Answers:**

DESIRE (Cards 1, 2, 22, 31, 40, 41, 42)  
LEARN (Cards 5, 6, 7, 8, 16, 17, 25, 26, 33, 34, 39)  
HOLY GHOST (Cards #11, 12, 13, 20, 21, 28, 29, 37, 38)  
PRAY (Cards 3, 4, 14, 15, 23, 24, 32)  
OBEY (Cards 9, 10, 18, 19, 27, 30, 35, 36)

| MOVE 1 | MOVE 2 | MOVE 3 | MOVE 1 | MOVE 2 | MOVE 3 | MOVE 1 | MOVE 2 | MOVE 3 |
| --- | --- | --- | --- | --- | --- | --- | --- | --- |
| MOVE 1 | MOVE 2 | MOVE 3 | MOVE 1 | MOVE 2 | MOVE 3 | MOVE 1 | MOVE 2 | MOVE 3 |
| MOVE 1 | MOVE 2 | MOVE 3 | MOVE 1 | MOVE 2 | MOVE 3 | MOVE 1 | MOVE 2 | MOVE 3 |
| MOVE 1 | MOVE 2 | MOVE 3 | MOVE 1 | MOVE 2 | MOVE 3 | MOVE 1 | MOVE 2 | MOVE 3 |

**TESTIMONY CARD #1:** We _____ to gain a stronger testimony of the gospel of Jesus Christ.

**TESTIMONY CARD #2:** This _____ helps us want to work to receive a testimony.

**TESTIMONY CARD #3:** We _____ to Heavenly Father and tell him of our desire to know that Jesus Christ is our Savior

**TESTIMONY CARD #4:** We can _____ to know that the gospel is true.

**TESTIMONY CARD #5:** We _____ about Jesus and what he wants us to do.

**TESTIMONY CARD #6:** As we read the scriptures we _____ about Jesus.

**TESTIMONY CARD #7:** We _____ about Jesus by attending family home evening, Primary, and sacrament meeting.

**TESTIMONY CARD #8:** We _____ about Jesus by listening to our parents, teachers, the living prophet, and other righteous leaders.

**TESTIMONY CARD #9:** If we want to know the gospel of Jesus Christ is true, we _____ (which means to live it).

**TESTIMONY CARD #10:** We _____ the commandments and follow the teachings of Jesus.

**TESTIMONY CARD #11:** Our testimonies come to us through the _____ _____.

**TESTIMONY CARD #12:** The _____ _____ speaks to our hearts and minds.

**TESTIMONY CARD #13:**
The _____ _____ lets us know within ourselves that the gospel is true.

**TESTIMONY CARD #14:**
We _____ in the name of Jesus Christ.

**TESTIMONY CARD #15:**
I will search, ponder, and _____ about the scriptures each day.

**TESTIMONY CARD #16:**
When you go to school, listen and _____ to get a good education.

**TESTIMONY CARD #17:**
As we _____ of Nephi's courage, we find it easy to choose the right.

**TESTIMONY CARD #18:**
I do what my parents say. This way I am learning to _____.

**TESTIMONY CARD #19:**
I will do what the prophets say. This means I will _____.

**TESTIMONY CARD #20:**
I am not alone. Jesus sent the _____ _____ to comfort me.

**TESTIMONY CARD #21:**
The _____ _____ tells me what I need to change.

**TESTIMONY CARD #22:**
The _____ to be healthy makes us want to live the Word of Wisdom.

**TESTIMONY CARD #23:**
_____ to be an example to others. Each day, show them how to live the righteous way.

**TESTIMONY CARD #24:**
James 1:5 tells us to _____ to "ask of God" if something is true.

**TESTIMONY CARD #25:**
When a family _____s together, a family stays together.

**TESTIMONY CARD #26:**
What you _____ in this life is a heavenly treasure, something you can take with you when you die.

**TESTIMONY CARD #27:**
The more we _____ about the gospel of Jesus Christ, the happier we feel.

**TESTIMONY CARD #28:**
When I partake of the sacrament on the Sabbath day, I promise to _____.

**TESTIMONY CARD #29:**
The _____ _____ is my guide. He is my spirit's guide.

**TESTIMONY CARD #30:**
The happy feeling in my heart, lets me know the _____ _____ is there for me.

**TESTIMONY CARD #31:**
Each time I pray, I learn new ways to _____.

**TESTIMONY CARD #32:**
The _____ to show gratitude helps us say, "Thank you."

**TESTIMONY CARD #33:**
Reading the scriptures helps us _____ to be happy.

**TESTIMONY CARD #34:**
I kneel to _____ every day to thank Heavenly Father and say what is in my heart.

**TESTIMONY CARD #35:**
We _____ about our ancestors when we do our family history.

**TESTIMONY CARD #36:**
As we _____ to make good choices, we can stay on heaven's straight and narrow path.

**TESTIMONY CARD #37:**
I will _____, which means to choose the righteous way.

**TESTIMONY CARD #38:**
When I say OK, this means I will _____.

**TESTIMONY CARD #39:**
The still small voice of the _____ _____ teaches me to know the truth.

**TESTIMONY CARD #40:**
The _____ _____ is my true, eternal friend.

**TESTIMONY CARD #41:**
_____ to be kind, to love others as Jesus did.

**TESTIMONY CARD #42:**
Because we _____ to share the gospel, we bear our testimony.

Primary Partners Teaching Tools — I Belong to The Church — Theme 12

# Theme 12: His Truth I Will Proclaim—Mosiah 18:9

**SONG:** Sing "I Want to Be a Missionary Now," page 168, and "We'll Bring the World His Truth," page 172, in the *Children's Songbook*.

Ask: "How can we gain and share a testimony of the gospel of Jesus Christ?"
Answer the question using the scriptures, Primary lessons, and sources below to teach.

> **What Is a Testimony? I Can Have a Testimony of Jesus Christ, His Gospel, and His Church**
> (D&C 76:22; *Primary 4*, lessons 33, 44; *Primary 5*, lesson 46).

## Sharing Time Activity 1:

I Will Be Valiant and Testify of Jesus (Valiant Testimony Balloon Maze)

**TO MAKE:** *Copy, color, and cut out the *Valiant Testimony Balloon Maze* (page 127).

**PREPARATION:** Review lesson 43, the attention activity (page 151), and enrichment activity 2 (page 153) in the *Primary 7 New Testament Manual*.

**ACTIVITY:** Help children learn how they can acquire a valiant testimony that can help them testify of Jesus Christ and His plan of salvation. Have children find the missing letters that go in the word box by drawing a line (with different colored crayons, pencils, or markers) to the balloon. Unscramble missing letters and place them in the word box to learn ways you can be valiant.

*All images can be printed in full color or black and white using the CD-ROM: *Primary Partners Teaching Tools—I Belong to The Church of Jesus Christ of Latter-day Saints*.

Primary Partners Teaching Tools — I Belong to The Church — Theme 12

**I Can Share the Gladness of the Gospel with Others**
(D&C 84:62; *Primary 2*, lesson 11; *Primary 4*, lesson 17).

**Sharing Time Activity 2:** I Will Prepare Now to Share the Gospel with Others (Missionary Mystery! Word Search)

**TO MAKE:** *Copy and color the *Missionary Mystery! Word Search* (page 128). Bring a pencil.
**PREPARATION:** Review lesson 44 and discussion: "What steps have you taken and can take in the future to share the gospel?" See page 156 in the *Primary 7 New Testament Manual*.
**ACTIVITY:** Have children help you complete this word search to learn ways they can prepare for a mission now and in the future. Follow instructions on the word search.

**Sharing Time Activity 3:**
I Will Prepare for My Mission (Missionary Doors Scripture Search)

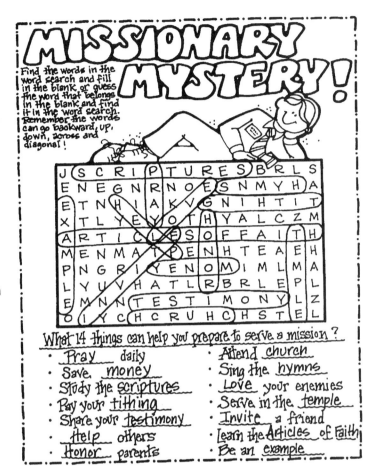

**TO MAKE:** *Copy, color, and cut out the *Missionary Doors Scripture Search* (page 129).
**PREPARATION:** Review lesson 9 and enrichment activity 4 (page 37) in the *Primary 6 Old Testament Manual*.
**ACTIVITY:** Help children learn five ways they can prepare now to share the gospel on a full-time mission when they are older. Have children take turns reading the scriptures and fill in the missing words.
**Answers:** Mosiah 18:13 (keep covenants), D&C 38:42 (be clean), Acts 11:26 (go to church), Matthew 22:29 (study scriptures), and D&C 48:4 (save money).

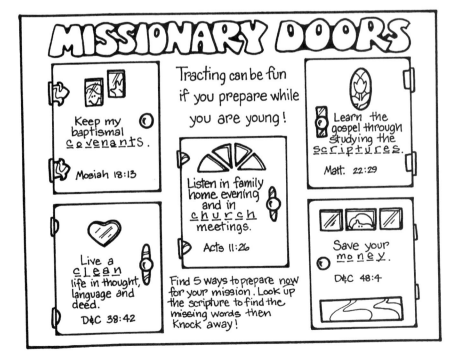

*All images can be printed in full color or black and white using the CD-ROM: *Primary Partners Teaching Tools—I Belong to The Church of Jesus Christ of Latter-day Saints*.

**I Can Prepare to Be a Missionary Now** (1 Timothy 4:12; *Primary 3*, lesson 25; *Primary 6*, lesson 9).

**Sharing Time Activity 4:** Heavenly Father Wants Everyone to Learn the Gospel (My Mission Statement Message Decoder)

**TO MAKE:** *Copy and color the *My Mission Statement Message Decoder* (page 130).
**PREPARATION:** Review lesson 40 and enrichment activity 2 (page 141) in the *Primary 7 New Testament Manual*.
**ACTIVITY:** The song "We'll Bring the World His Truth" (page 172 in *Children's Songbook*) contains clues to the mission statement. Help children learn how they can be missionaries by printing the letters of the pictured objects to decode the message "I will learn and teach the gospel of Jesus Christ." Tell children that Jesus Christ had to learn the gospel before He taught it. We too must learn all we can about the gospel of Jesus Christ. As we learn something about the gospel from our teachers and reading the scriptures, let's share what we learn with others. Sharing the gospel and living the gospel is the best way to gain and keep our testimony. Jesus' testimony grew each day because He learned about the gospel and shared His testimony with others. Our testimony can grow each day. We can "increase in wisdom" as Jesus did. Read Luke 2:52.

**I Am Grateful for the Savior and the Blessings of My Membership in His Church**
(Mosiah 2:41; *Primary 1*, lesson 42; *Primary 3*, lesson 21).

**Sharing Time Activity 5:** I Can "Bear" My Testimony (Secret Message Poster)

**TO MAKE:** *Copy and color the *Secret Message Poster* (page 131). Bring a pencil.
**PREPARATION:** Review lesson 37 and enrichment activity 1 (page 129) in the *Primary 7 New Testament Manual*.
**ACTIVITY:** Let children discover the secret message on their own to learn what to say when they "bear" their testimony. Using the words in the message below, fill in the blanks. *Answers* (shown left: know, of, is, Jesus Christ, true, gospel, the).

# MISSIONARY MYSTERY!

Find the words in the word search and fill in the blank, or guess the word that belongs in the blank and find it in the word search. Remember the words can go backward, up, down, across and diagonal!

```
J S C R I P T U R E S B R L S
E N E G N R N O E S N M Y H A
E T N H I A K V G N I H T I T
X T L Y E Y O T H Y A L C Z M
A R T I C L E S O F F A I T H
M E N M A T P E N H T E A E H
P N G R I Y E N O M I M L M A
L Y U V H A T L R B R L E P L
E M N N T E S T I M O N Y L Z
O I Y C H C R U H C H S T E L
```

## What 14 things can help you prepare to serve a mission?

- _____ daily
- Save _____
- Study the _____
- Pay your _____
- Share your _____
- _____ others
- _____ parents
- Attend _____
- Sing the _____
- _____ your enemies
- Serve in the _____
- _____ a friend
- Learn the _____
- Be an _____

# MISSIONARY DOORS

Learn the gospel through studying the _ _ _ _ _ _
Matt. 22:29

Save your _ _ _ _
D&C 48:4

Tracting can be fun if you prepare while you are young!

Listen in family home evening and in _ _ _ _ _ _ meetings.
Acts 11:26

Keep my baptismal _ _ _ _ _ _ _ S.
Mosiah 18:13

Live a _ _ _ _ life in thought, language and deed.
D&C 38:42

Find 5 ways to prepare now for your mission. Look up the scripture to find the missing words then knock away!

# My Mission Statement

To learn how you can be a missionary, print the letters of the pictured objects to decode the message.

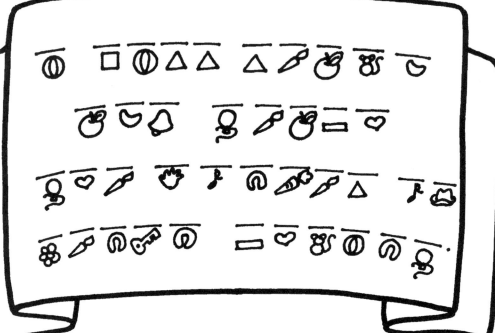

# Preview of Primary Partners Sharing Time 2003 book and CD-ROM

## I Belong to The Church of Jesus Christ of Latter-day Saints
### Activities to Use for Sharing Time and Family Home Evenings

- 12 Learning Activities that teach the gospel
- 12 Bite-size Memorize Scripture Posters
- Preview of 66 more Learning Activities (Teaching Tools)

---

"I Belong to The Church of Jesus Christ of Latter-day Saints"
Sharing Time Themes 1-12

1. I Belong to The Church of Jesus Christ
2. I Belong to The Church of Jesus Christ of Latter-day Saints
3. I Know Who I Am
4. I Believe in the Savior, Jesus Christ
5. The Prophet Speaks for the Savior. I Can Follow the Prophet Today.
6. I Know God's Plan
7. I'll Follow Him in Faith
8. I'll Honor His Name
9. I'll Do What Is Right
10. I'll Follow His Light
11. Teachings of the Prophet
12. His Truth I Will Proclaim

# Enjoy Full-color, Ready-to-use Presentations:

## Gospel Fun Activities
Quick-and-Easy Family Home Evenings and Sharing Time

## Book 1: Super Singing Activities
## Book 2: Super Little Singers
to Motivate Children to Sing

In minutes you can teach a child basic principles of the gospel from these post-and-present games and activities.

Since a picture is worth 1,000 words, we have created the visuals that will help you teach the gospel with very little effort. These teaching tools are easy to present. Simply mount them on a poster, board, or wall. Children enjoy creating and presenting the activities, so put them in charge whenever you can.

The visuals are ready to cut out, post and present, helping you teach the following gospel subjects: accountability, choose the right, commandments, faith, follow Jesus, the Holy Ghost, missionary talents, missionary Work, repentance, Second Coming, service, and testimony.

All of the visuals can also be printed in color or black and white using the *Gospel Fun Activities* CD-ROM.

With these two volumes of singing activities, there is never a dull moment in Primary and family home evening.

Use them each week along with the *Primary Partners Singing Fun!* book and CD-ROM to match the sharing time theme for the current year.

With these colored, ready-to-use visuals you can create a memorable singing experience. All of the visuals in the two books can be printed from the CD-ROM in color or black and white.

Some of the activities in *Super Singing Activities* are: Melody's Family Tree, Bird in the Leafy Treetops, Build a Snowman, Christmas Tree Sing with Me, City of Enoch Singing Meter, Fill Noah's Ark Pick-a-Song (shown right), and more.

In the *Super Little Singers* you will find visuals or actions for 28 songs, plus six singing motivators. You will find: I Sing Like a Bird singing motivator, action activities, visuals for seven all-time favorite children's songs, e.g., "Ants Go Marching," Eensy Weensy Spider," "Five Little Ducks," "Five Little Speckled Frogs," "Old MacDonald," "Twinkle, Twinkle, Little Star," "Wheels on the Bus," and twenty-one other songs from the *Children's Songbook*.

# More 2003 Sharing Time Theme Books and CD-ROMS:
## Theme: "I Belong to The Church of Jesus Christ of Latter-day Saints"

| 2003 Themes | Primary Partners Sharing Time book and CD-ROM | Gospel Fun Activities all-color book and CD-ROM | Primary Partners Singing Fun! book and CD-ROM |
|---|---|---|---|
| 1. I Belong to The Church of Jesus Christ | 1. Beginning—Apostasy Time Line Show-and-Tell | | 1. "The Church of Jesus Christ" |
| 2. I Belong to The Church of Jesus Christ of Latter-day Saints | 2. Restoration—Latter-days Time Line Show-and-Tell | | 2. "On a Golden Springtime" |
| 3. I Know Who I Am | 3. Because I Am a Child of God Match Game | | 3. "I Am a Child of God" |
| 4. I Believe in the Savior Jesus Christ | 4. I Will Follow Jesus Puzzle Quiz | 4. Use Activity 9: Happy Henry and Miserable Mac Body Building Puzzles. | 4. "Easter Hosanna" |
| 5. The Prophet Speaks for the Savior. I Can Follow Him | 5. The Apostles Testify Seek-and-Say | | 5. "The Things I Do" |
| 6. I Know God's Plan | 6. Agency Actions Consequences Countenance Game | 6. Use Activities 1: Annabell's Accountable Cow Farm, 2: CTR Tools Match Game, 3: Commandment Maze, 10: Second Coming Suitcase. | 6. "I Lived in Heaven" |
| 7. I'll Follow Him in Faith | 7. Anytime, Anywhere Prayer Maze | 7. Use Activities 4: Strong and Wilting Plant Match Game, 5: Find the Light Situation Spotlight. | 7. "Lord, I Would Follow Thee" |
| 8. I'll Honor His Name | 8. Children Around the World Honor Jesus | 8. Use Activities 1, 2, and 3 (see #6 above). | 8. "Choose the Right Way" |
| 9. I'll Do What is Right | 9. Holy Ghost Guides, Feelings Finder | 9. Use Activity 6: Trail to Holy Ghost Town Game. | |
| 10. I'll Follow His Light | 10. Facing the Sun/Son Stories of Jesus | 10. Use Activities 4 and 5 (see #7 above), 11: My Service Garden Game to Plant Acts of Service. | |
| 11. Teachings of the Prophet | 11. Blessings Brainstorm | | |
| 12. His Truth I Will Proclaim | 12. Stand as a Witness Testimony Time | 12. Use Activities 7: Missionary Kite Maze, 8: Missionary Fish Find, 12: Testimony Foundation | |

# Theme 1. I Belong to The Church of Jesus Christ

**ACTIVITY:** Church Beginning—Apostasy Time Line Show-and-Tell

**OBJECTIVE:** Help children realize that the gospel of Jesus Christ was on the earth at one time, and then taken away. Children can learn about being with Jesus and Heavenly Father in the premortal life and then following Heavenly Father's plan which brought us to earth. Having the gospel is a great blessing.

# 2. I Belong to The Church of Jesus Christ of Latter-day Saints

**ACTIVITY:** Restoration-Latter-days Time Line Show-and-Tell

**OBJECTIVE:** Help children learn about the period of darkness to the time the Church was restored by the Prophet Joseph Smith in the Latter-days. All of the important parts of the gospel that were taken away at the time of the apostasy are now restored for us today. The Church of Jesus Christ (of Latter-day Saints) will remain on the earth. It will not be taken away again.

# Theme 3. I Know Who I Am

**ACTIVITY:** Because I Am a Child of God Match Game

**OBJECTIVE:** Help children realize how special they are, that they are children of God who has a purpose for their life. The Gospel of Jesus Christ gives them that purpose.

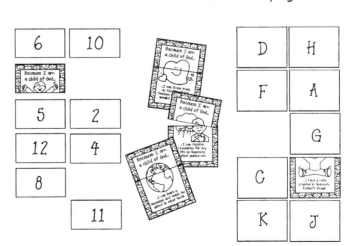

# Theme 4. I Believe in the Savior, Jesus Christ

**ACTIVITY:** I Have Faith in Jesus Christ Storyboard

**OBJECTIVE:** Help children learn the stories of Jesus so that they will know that He is the Savior.

# Theme 5. The Prophet Speaks for the Savior. I Can Follow the Prophet Today

**ACTIVITY:** Post a Prophet Clue Game

**OBJECTIVE:** Help children learn of prophets who spoke for the Savior, who testified of Him.

# Theme 6. I Know God's Plan

**ACTIVITY:** Consequences Countenance Game

**OBJECTIVE:** Help children realize that each choice they make has a consequence that affects the way we feel. Our feelings show on our face, changing our countenance.

# Theme 7. I'll Follow Him in Faith

**ACTIVITY:** Anytime, Anywhere Prayer True Storyboard

**OBJECTIVE:** Read true stories on prayer to help children know that they don't need to be by their bedside to pray; they can pray anytime, and anywhere to seek Heavenly Father's guidance.

# Theme 8. I'll Honor His Name

**ACTIVITY:** Children Around the World Honor Jesus

**OBJECTIVE:** Help children look at different situations and try to guess how people in these stories honored Jesus.

# Theme 9. I'll Do What Is Right

**ACTIVITY:** The Holy Ghost Will Guide Me Invite the Spirit Choices Game

**OBJECTIVE:** Help children learn to make choices that invite the Spirit of the Holy Ghost.

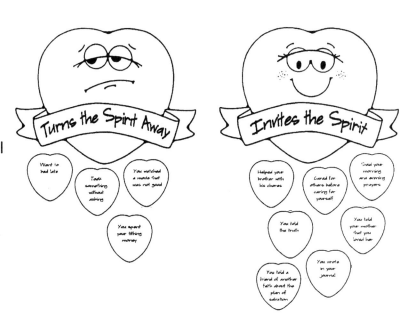

# Theme 10. I'll Follow His Light

**ACTIVITY:** Facing the Sun/Son Stories of Jesus

**OBJECTIVE:** Help children know the importance of following Jesus Christ, the Son of God to help our testimonies grow, just as the sunflowers face the sun to grow.

# Theme 11. Teachings of the Prophet

**ACTIVITY:** Blessings Brainstorm

**OBJECTIVE:** Help children view images that remind them of ways they can follow the prophet and the blessings that come from following him.

# Theme 12. His Truth I Will Proclaim

**ACTIVITY:** Stand as a Witness Testimony Time

**OBJECTIVE:** Encourage children to think about and bear their testimony about specific gospel subjects.